SO-BZD-390

You Are My Friends

Gospel Reflections for Your Spiritual Journey

YOU Are My FRIENDS

Gospel Reflections for Your Spiritual Journey

JOSEPH STOUTZENBERGER

TWENTY THIRD 23rd
PUBLICATIONS

Dedication

To my extended family,
the students at Holy Family University,
who show me many faces of Christ

Acknowledgment

I would like to thank Fr. John Bohrer for his help with this book, especially for suggesting reflection questions. He pushed me not to be overly academic, for which I am grateful.

Twenty-Third Publications / A Division of Bayard
One Montauk Avenue, Suite 200
New London, CT 06320
(860) 437-3012 or (800) 321-0411
www.23rdpublications.com

Copyright ©2007 Joseph Stoutzenberger. All rights reserved. No part of this publication may be reproduced in any manner without prior written permission of the publisher. Write to the Permissions Editor.

Unless otherwise noted, the Scripture passages contained herein are from the *New Revised Standard Version of the Bible*, copyright ©1989, by the Division of Christian Education of the National Council of Churches in the U.S.A. All rights reserved.

ISBN 978-1-58595-551-0

Library of Congress Catalog Card Number: 2005935878
Printed in the U.S.A.

Contents

Introduction

Even Mary Magdalene didn't recognize him at first. She thought he was a gardener. Despite his Resurrection and his assurances that he is with us always, Jesus can be elusive—even now and even to his closest friends. Churches honoring him dot our landscape; festivals in his name mark off our weeks and years. He is constantly appealed to in public conversation. Nevertheless, we still seem to miss him.

I discovered this firsthand not so long ago. When another teacher became ill, I inherited his course, "Jesus the Christ." I approached the subject as an academic study—pouring out information, offering insights from scholars, raising questions, and developing "critical thinking." During the course students learned, for example, that the accounts of Jesus' birth contain little that scholars can verify as factual history. The students also learned that many things attributed to Jesus were no doubt added to the gospels, or at least edited, years after his death. I began to fear that this strictly academic approach to Jesus might be undermining their faith, which was already under attack from countless forces in the world around them. Students were certainly getting to know more about Jesus, but they weren't being helped to know Jesus.

The students were astute enough to realize that they wanted more from the course. While they appreciated learning new information and theories about Jesus, they also wanted to connect what they were studying to their everyday lives. They wanted to meet the Jesus who makes a difference. Otherwise, what is the point? Why not have a course on, say, Julius Caesar or Napoleon instead? I can still hear students' questions. "Since Jesus sided with the outcasts of his day, shouldn't we try to figure out who the outcasts of our day are?" "Did Jesus tell stories to make his message simple and clear, or does he actually want us to make sense of them for ourselves?" "Did Jesus have feelings, suffer pain, and experience emotional hurts just like us?" "What does Jesus offer us, and what does he want of us?"

I began writing reflections on topics discussed in class. I wrote them for myself initially. I didn't want to get so bogged down in an academic study of Jesus that I missed his personal message to me. On occasion, I gave my reflections to the students who seemed interested. One student shared some of my reflections with her parish prayer group, who wanted more of the same. I offered these reflections as invitations to spend time with Jesus. In these reflections, Jesus is not an object of study but a friend who wants to share our lives. I gathered my reflections together in this book with that same offer.

Nearly one-third of the world's population believes that Jesus Christ is the Son of God, the Savior of the world. Despite this fact, so many of us know little about him beyond fleeting images: his birth in a stable, his death on the cross, certain stories and miracles. Our relationship with Jesus can easily get lost amid the distractions and attractions of modern life. Nonetheless, an inner longing may spark the desire to make our relationship with Jesus deeper, stronger, and more constant.

If we search for ways to feed our hunger for Jesus, simply picking up a Bible and reading it can overwhelm us. We can meet the word of God in the written word, but only if we ponder the ways it speaks to our lives. The earliest Christians never had written gospels to sustain them as we do. Their Scriptures were the stories of their encounters with Christ, which they shared over the Eucharist. Then as now, the word of God is meant to be a living word whose home is our hearts, a word savored in our minds, a word lived moment by moment.

St. Teresa of Avila reminds us that prayer is an intimate conversation with a friend. This little book is designed to help with that conversation. The gospel passages begin the exchange. The reflections then leapfrog from the message of Jesus in the gospels to present-day concerns. The reflections link together two sources of wisdom: the gospels and our lives. Through this conversation, Jesus becomes more alive and more tangible, thereby helping us deepen our relationship with him. If we read the gospels prayerfully, then we can also read the newspaper, a child's report card, e-mails from friends, and other daily occurrences prayerfully, too.

You will notice journal-like lines at various points throughout the book. This space is provided for your personal responses to the question Jesus asks his friends, "And who do *you* say I am?"

Mark's gospel sets out to tell us "the good news of Jesus Christ, the Son of God" (1:1). May we each find good news in our encounters with Jesus.

When Jesus turned and saw them following, he said to them,
"What are you looking for?" They said to him, "Rabbi"
(which translated means Teacher), "where are you staying?"
He said to them, "Come and see."
JOHN 1:38–39

1

Sharing the Journey

I do not call you servants any longer, because the servant
does not know what the master is doing;
but I have called you friends.
JOHN 15:15

E ach of us could use another friend. Someone always there for
us, whose very presence frees us to be ourselves. Someone
who shares our deepest and darkest secrets, who forgives our
faults and overlooks our shortcomings. Someone who challenges
us without attacking us. Someone without whom life just wouldn't
be the same.

Why not consider Jesus as that friend? Before dismissing the idea
as religious nonsense, know that the gospels tell us that Jesus wants
to be such a friend. In fact, he can be our best friend. Of course,
Jesus isn't physically present to us the way other friends are.
Nonetheless, he knows our inmost thoughts and loves us uncondi-
tionally. He told the people of his day that his heavenly Father cares
for every sparrow and that each person was worth more than many
sparrows. Jesus' message wasn't meant only for the people of his
day; he has the same message for us today. We are unique and special and loveable in God's eyes.

We may find that we are overly attentive to the way we look. Perhaps we fixate on our hair. Perhaps we focus on our eyes or a pesky skin blemish that looks particularly noticeable at the worst possible moment. We might focus on what we see as shortcomings in our social or intellectual skills. Jesus sees us in a way that no mirror can reveal. To Jesus, we are beautiful—externally, and more importantly, deep down.

What a difference it could make if we actually heard his message! Chances are, if we did hear it, we would never be arrogant or snobbish or look down on others as inferior. Rather, we would marvel at who we are and at what we can offer to others. Although our struggles to fit in and be at home in the world wouldn't end, we wouldn't feel so alone. We would have someone behind us—indeed, within us—who can help us through our struggles. If we spent time with Jesus, he would remind us to look at what really matters, namely that ultimately our lives are in God's hands and that we live under God's loving gaze.

Buddhists tell a story of a man searching for his ox. He looks here, there, and everywhere to no avail. He holds out hope because, despite his frustration, he occasionally notices ox droppings and ox hoofprints. On the edge of despair, he finally discovers that he has been riding his ox all along.

Many religious traditions have stories with a similar theme. The Footprints poem talks about a person who is carried by God along a sandy shore unaware of God's presence. Jesus told a story about a father who climbed a hill every day, anxiously peering across the fields for signs of his wayward son's return. If we look within and search our hearts, we may discover that we are not alone.

We shouldn't get discouraged at setbacks in our friendship with Jesus. As in any relationship, we are likely to experience both honeymoon periods and dark times as well. The point is that Jesus is always waiting for us. In other words, he is already our best friend. Isn't it worth cultivating this friendship?

≋ Reflect

- *Recall an experience of true friendship you have had. What was it like? What did it require on your part?*

- *If you were to cultivate a friendship with Jesus, what might this require of you? What three things would you be willing to do to make such a friendship work?*

- *Do you presently make time in your day for prayer (conversation with Jesus)? What form does this take? What do you hope for from this experience?*

🖊 Your Thoughts

2

Hidden Treasure

The kingdom of heaven is like treasure hidden in a field,
which someone found and hid; then in his joy
he goes and sells all that he has and buys that field.
MATTHEW 13:44

When was the last time you weren't doing something? Watching television doesn't count. Sitting at a computer, even if you think about other things, is also doing something. Most of us today have precious little downtime. Keeping busy is a modern addiction. We are more likely to suffer from chronic busyness than from idleness. We take little time to see or listen, to laugh or cry. Children can play in the snow for hours. As we get older, we often enjoy the wonders of a snowfall for minutes rather than hours, only to return home and watch a movie we've seen numerous times. We might be momentarily struck by a beautiful sunset but quickly pass it by to go on about our business.

If we fail to set aside quiet time, time to enter the quiet space within us, we miss out on hidden treasure. One primary way to cultivate a relationship with Jesus is simply to journey within ourselves. Surprisingly, looking within is something few people do. Our culture dictates against it. We contend with blaring televisions, radios, and computer screens in restaurants, doctors' offices, and car repair shops. Rather than peace and quiet, our homes often resonate with noise intruding from the outside world. Even if we attend church services, we are treated to only a few moments of silence.

The night before he died, Jesus invited his apostles to stay awake with him, to spend time in prayer. What would happen if we set aside a few minutes to sit alone in silence and imagine that Jesus is sitting next to us? We might use the time to speak with Jesus, a simple form of prayer that may be beneficial. If our minds wander to recent or upcoming events, then we can ask Jesus to help us see the events through his eyes. If we spend quiet time with Jesus at the start of the day, we could thank him for what is to come. This prayer would help us approach the day with an entirely fresh attitude—like getting into the habit of eating a healthy breakfast and arriving at work or school early. If we spend quiet time with Jesus late at night, we might find that the burdens we carried all day long are not as heavy as they seem. This night prayer is like getting a good night's sleep. It can calm us and rejuvenate us for the next day's adventure.

The opportunity to pause, to look within our hearts, and to settle in with Jesus for a while can bring needed peace in the midst of the storms that surround us. We can dismiss time with Jesus as worthwhile but impossible to fit into our busy schedule. Although Jesus' presence within us may go unnoticed or be taken for granted, isn't an encounter with him worth sacrificing for? If we search for Jesus within, hidden treasure awaits us.

≋ Reflect

- *How successful are you at balancing busyness and downtime in your life?*

- *How might you use your downtime to focus on your relationship with Jesus?*

- *What prayer practices help you stay awake with Jesus?*

3

God Loves Stories

*I will open my mouth to speak in parables; I will proclaim
what has been hidden from the foundation of the world.*
MATTHEW 13:35

"A man was going down from Jerusalem to Jericho, and fell into the hands of robbers…" (Lk 10:30). As soon as we hear these words, we are drawn into a story filled with suspense. What will happen to the man? How badly will he be hurt? Will anyone rescue him? Jesus created this tale to get across a profound but startling message: help comes from the least likely places. Samaritans were not supposed to be good people, and a Galilean carpenter turned wandering preacher (Jesus) was not supposed to be the Savior of the world.

Traditional Jewish wisdom states: "God made human beings because God loves stories." Certainly Jesus was attuned to the power of stories. Jesus told stories that have deep and often unexpected meanings. To symbolize how seriously they took a story's message, there are ancient accounts about listeners actually eating the scrolls on which the stories were written. Do we "chew" on the stories of Jesus and digest them? Chewing takes time and reflection. If we carry Jesus' stories within us, we might find that a message contained in one of them pops into our consciousness just when we need it most.

In one gospel story, Jesus comes upon a crowd about to stone a woman to death. The crowd accuses her of adultery. Jesus' well-known admonition to the crowd is, "Let anyone among you who is without sin be the first to throw a stone at her" (Jn 8:7). If we are constantly ready to hurl stones at public leaders, teachers, or the people with whom we live or work, we would do well to tap into this story for guidance. On the other hand, if we find others throwing stones at us, we have plenty of Jesus' stories to support us. For example, we certainly can imagine what it feels like to be a lost sheep. Jesus says that a good shepherd is one who has a hundred sheep, but leaves the ninety-nine to search for the one sheep that is missing. Actually, this is not sensible shepherding. A sensible shepherd stays with the ninety-nine, keeping them together lest others wander off. Jesus' shepherd is good, not sensible. Jesus defies common sense to tell us that even when we feel lost and abandoned, he will find us.

The woman in adultery and the lost sheep are just two examples of Jesus' stories worth making part of our repertoire of mental images. Lost coins, a young man eating slop from a pigpen, a great banquet, and vines overflowing with delicious grapes are other images from Jesus that we can add to the storehouse of our consciousness. As with any great work of art or literature, we should savor the gospel stories, allowing them to astonish us.

≋ Reflect

- *Which gospel stories have put you in closer touch with Jesus?*

- *What is your favorite story about Jesus? Does this story make it easier for you to place your trust in Jesus, to rely on him in daily ways? Why or why not?*

- *What are some things you might say to Jesus in prayer after reading your favorite gospel story?*

4

A Joyful Life

I have said these things to you so that my joy may be in you,
and that your joy may be complete.
JOHN 15:11

Many people look back on their teen years as the most
intense time of their lives. The thrill of a first kiss, a cham-
pionship season, or a summer romance at camp is hard
to beat. There is also a dark side to such intensity. We can be devas-
tated when our first love turns sour or when we are cut from the team
we have set our hopes on. The teen years can be a roller coaster of
emotions. As we grow older, we often look back longingly on that
time when we felt so strongly about life.

What does Jesus say about the intense feelings that come with our
humanity? Unfortunately, we tend to associate religion with restraint,
holding back, and keeping our emotions in check. Jesus was not an
ascetic who shunned pleasure; he didn't call for self-denial for its own
sake. In fact, he was notorious for enjoying meals with all kinds of
people. If we look at the gospels, we discover more references to joy
than to pain, suffering, and sadness. Our joy is what Jesus wants; our
suffering is what he promises to overcome. During his time of active
ministry he lived a very intense life. Jesus did more than his share of

both weeping and rejoicing. He felt deeply those things that make life worth living and worth sacrificing for. He used a striking image to illustrate his understanding of joy—childbirth (Jn 16:21). We, too, experience pain and suffering. When we experience the pain that comes from giving ourselves, this pain leads to new life, just as it does in childbirth. Jesus modeled his message: grasping onto things leads to sadness while sharing brings happiness.

What would a prescription for a joyful life include? Would the prescription resemble the one Jesus mapped out in his life and teaching? Would it list, "Love others as you love yourself" and "Pray for those who persecute you"? Would the alternatives, "Hate your enemies" and "Get even," make your life more satisfying? In our culture, we tend to view "getting" as the way to happiness. Getting a new car, getting that great house, or getting the woman or man of our dreams is supposed to make us happy. Jesus suggests "letting go" as the way to true happiness. Whatever his life was like in the carpenter shop in Nazareth, he gave it up to pursue a more challenging goal. He let go of whatever creature comforts he had in order to make himself available to people in need. He opened people's eyes to a new way of being together; joy is found through community sharing rather than through hoarding and grasping.

Do we need to stop what we are doing in order to be joyful? A brief scene from the gospels suggests that we can discover Jesus and do his work as we go about our daily life. In Matthew 24:41, two women are grinding grain together. Both are doing the same work. However, one woman recognizes the coming of the Son of Man; the other woman does not. The difference? The first woman is "awake." Being awake to God's love for us in Christ Jesus makes our own daily grind more joyful. We may be a society of pleasure seekers, but we seem to miss out on joy. Jesus is not anti-pleasure, but he has something much greater in mind for us—joy. His prescription for joy offers a needed counter-balance to the very different set of values dominant in our culture. In the end, isn't the "Jesus prescription" the true way to happiness?

≋ Reflect

- *Can you think of people who exhibit joy because of what they believe? What do you think is their source of joy?*

- *What brings you spiritual joy? In what ways do you experience this in your prayer?*

- *What would be your prescription for a joyful life? How is your prescription similar to that of Jesus?*

Your Thoughts

5

The Spirit of Wonder

A centurion came to him, saying, "Lord, my servant is lying at home paralyzed, in terrible distress....I am not worthy to have you come under my roof; but only speak the word, and my servant will be healed...." When Jesus heard him, he was amazed.
MATTHEW 8:5–6, 8, 10

One day an eighteenth-century Parisian priest noticed two teenage girls gesturing to each other in animated fashion. Observing their silent exchanges, he realized that they were deaf but that they were communicating with their hands as clearly and as forcefully as others do with spoken words. Although he was a highborn Frenchman and these were peasant girls, the priest said to them, "Teach me." In time, the priest, Abbe de L'Eppe, codified what the girls taught him into sign language and opened the first public school for people who are deaf.

We might believe that Abbe de L'Eppe did what any good Christian would do in his circumstances. Actually he was not supported in his work; at the time most people failed to see the point of working with deaf people. Deaf people were beyond the pale of salvation. It was even questioned whether or not deaf people had souls! In the two deaf girls, Abbe de L'Eppe saw what others failed to see. He saw because he was blessed with a spirit of wonder, openness to viewing things differently, and the courage to challenge commonly held beliefs. He didn't take things for granted.

The gospels report an incident that parallels Abbe de L'Eppe's story. Typically, first-century Jews viewed Roman soldiers as incapable of faith, just as eighteenth-century Parisians believed deaf people were incapable of conversation. Jesus was amazed, astonished, and filled with wonder when a centurion realized that Jesus could cure his servant. Both the centurion and Jesus shared openness to the new insights that make faith possible. The ability to wonder underlies all faith.

In the course of our daily busyness we can miss much. The renowned twentieth-century rabbi Abraham Joshua Heschel suggested that, "what we lack is not a will to believe but a will to wonder." He described the Sabbath as a day set aside specifically to get us out of our business-as-usual mentality and into a spirit of wonder and reverence. The American Catholic monk Thomas Merton wrote that one of his most profound religious experiences occurred on a busy street corner while waiting for a doctor's appointment. Merton was overwhelmed by the utter beauty of the people passing by; he realized then and there that everyone is interconnected, one with another. Merton achieved this fresh insight because he possessed a sense of wonder. To believe in God is to believe that life is filled with endless surprises. Jesus himself was capable of wonder and amazement. Are we?

≋ Reflect

- *Describe a time when you were filled with wonder. How did the experience affect your faith life?*

- *What would it be like to approach every new day with a spirit of wonder?*

- *Have you ever experienced "endless surprises" because of your faith in God? How would you describe these experiences?*

6

God's Body Language

And the Word became flesh and lived among us.
JOHN 1:14

One of the world's most beloved paintings is "The Angelus" by the nineteenth-century French painter Jean-François Millet. The picture depicts two peasant farmers pausing from their work as church bells in the distance chime the evening Angelus, a brief prayer centered on the phrase: "And the Word was made Flesh and dwelt among us." In traditional Catholic countries, the Angelus was once recited three times a day—morning, noon, and evening—to celebrate the great Christian mystery of the Incarnation, God's word become flesh.

The Angelus is a daily reminder that God shares our bodily existence and that we are to delight in our bodies. In other words, "body is bad, spirit is good" is a misreading of the gospels. Unfortunately, this message was one of the earliest heresies (false teachings) faced by Christianity, and this false teaching persists today. The very foundation of Christianity is an appreciation for and a celebration of the human condition as a unity of body and spirit. Christ is God in the flesh. Because of the mystery of the Incarnation, followers of Jesus viewed our participation in the bodily existence we share with him as special. Paulist Father

Thomas Ryan reminds us to reclaim the body in our spirituality. He sees potential for spiritual experience whenever we "cycle, swim, jog, dance, practice yoga, engage in manual labor, care for the earth, and make love."

From a Christian perspective, body and spirit are not as separate and distinct as they might appear; they support and enrich each other. Body makes spirit tangible; spirit makes the person more than just a collection of cells. In his first letter to the Christian community at Corinth, Paul clearly lays out the wonders of the body: "Do you not know that your bodies are members of Christ? Or do you not know that your body is a temple of the Holy Spirit within you...?" (1 Cor 6:15, 19). Because of his experience of Christ, Paul realizes how precious our bodies are. His image, "temple of the Holy Spirit," equates the body with the holiest of holy places that existed in all of Judaism—the Temple in Jerusalem. The Incarnation invites us to see others as precious and wondrous and our own bodies as sacred.

Where does a Christian understanding of the body take us? We come to a profound appreciation of the body. We do not "have" a body like we have a pair of jeans or sneakers. Rather, we are persons, body and soul. In all of our interactions with others, we are connecting person-to-person, not just body-to-body. When we forget that every person we meet is holy and that every body is a person whose depths reach the infinite, trouble results.

The way we treat other people reflects how we view the body. Certain ways of physical engagement with others flow from a sense of the preciousness of persons while other ways do not. Are you thinking only of sex here? Certainly, we need to be particularly attentive to sexual activity since sexual expression goes right to the core of our body-spirit human condition. However, we use our bodies in any number of creative and caring ways (just as there are many ways we can misuse our bodies and harm others and ourselves).

The word of God is an embodied word. It is Jesus Christ. It is also a word that dwells among us and within us. As we move about, encountering other people, we can welcome them with our bodies, shut them out, or even abuse them. Jesus wants us to be God's body language. It would be a shame to dim the light of God that shines through us, for we are temples of the Holy Spirit.

≋≋ Reflect

- *How could you feel more at home in your body? Have you ever discussed this with Jesus in prayer?*

- *What might you do to cultivate a "spirituality of the body" for yourself?*

- *What are some things you could do to reverence and respect others as embodied persons? In what ways can you include them in your prayer?*

Your Thoughts

7

Loving Ourselves

*See what love the Father has given us, that we should be
called children of God; and that is what we are.*
1 JOHN 3:1

I f we rank ourselves from one (very low self-esteem) to ten (very
high self-esteem), where would we be? How would our friends
and acquaintances rank themselves? Where would Jesus want us
to be on this scale—a "perfect ten" perhaps? Even in our age when
"love yourself" and "feel good about who you are" are akin to
national anthems, a majority of people see themselves closer to one
than ten. Concern for self-esteem and self-love sounds very modern, a by-product of psychology. By contrast, we tend to associate
the Christian message of love with loving others, not ourselves. In
the Christian tradition, self-love is often ignored, frowned upon, or
at best, taken for granted.

Part of the problem is that true self-love gets confused with its
false imitators. For example, self-love might be mistaken for arrogance and boasting. Self-love does not say, "I'm better than everyone else." Instead, a healthy sense of self-worth proclaims, "I'm glad
God made me who I am. I am someone precious in God's eyes, and
I treat myself accordingly." Jesus bases self-love on God's love for us.

If God cares for us so passionately, who are we not to love ourselves as well? Christian self-love is a necessary starting point for loving God in return and for loving others. Only when we love ourselves can we give the gift of ourselves to others.

One school of psychology uses simple terms to provide a balanced view. Both "I'm okay; you're not okay" (arrogance) and "I'm not okay; you're okay" (no sense of self-worth) are problem postures. Cultivating "I'm okay; you're okay" is the way to a wholesome self-image and healthy relationships. One Christian writer suggests that Scripture offers another intriguing position on the matter, namely: "I'm not okay; you're not okay, but that's okay." In other words, Jesus wants to assure those whose lives and self-perceptions are not okay that they are people of God-given worth who should reverence and celebrate themselves. In the words of a popular saying, "God doesn't make junk."

What is the path to loving ourselves as revealed by Jesus? The answer may at first appear contradictory. (Always expect confounding messages from Jesus!) True self-love manifests itself in forgetting about ourselves. Wondering whether or not people like us keeps us locked up inside ourselves. Fear of embarrassment or of making a mistake prevents us from laughing at and truly enjoying ourselves, warts and all. Loving ourselves leads to increased spontaneity and a free-spiritedness, to resilience in the face of setbacks. Self-love, which is really the same as accepting that God loves us, means being so comfortable in our own skins and with our unique personalities that we can focus on the needs and concerns of others.

Christian mystics invite us to nurture humility, a word related to "earth" and "humor." To be humble means to be real, honest about ourselves, possessing a healthy sense of our strengths and limitations. If we can laugh at ourselves in our earthiness, we are on the way to the self-love that mystics cultivate. Jesus himself says that if we are to be free we should learn from him, for he is "gentle and humble in heart" (Mt 11:29). We receive the grace to love ourselves and the courage to love others because God loves us. In other words, Jesus' message is: "Know yourself as a precious gift from God. Forget yourself and love in return."

≋ Reflect

- *How does it feel to know that God loves you so deeply? Are you more comfortable accepting yourself knowing this?*
- *Do you know anyone whom you would consider humble? Is humility an attractive quality to you? Why or why not?*
- *Complete this sentence: "If Jesus loves me, then…."*

Your Thoughts

8

Jesus and Oppression

The Spirit of the Lord is upon me...to bring good news to the poor. He has sent me to proclaim release to the captives and recovery of sight to the blind, to let the oppressed go free....
LUKE 4:18

After the 2004 presidential election, there was much discussion about the strong role religion played in the re-election of President Bush. Many Christians saw his election as a mandate for biblical values. People have differing views, however, about which biblical values are most important. A prominent evangelical Christian cut his Bible into pieces. He removed all the passages that referred to poverty and justice. His Bible was gutted, nearly empty. He tried to dramatize that by removing the cry for justice, we rob the Bible of its heart and soul.

Jesus brings salvation to the world—a core Christian belief. While salvation refers to heaven, life with God after death, salvation also means freedom from oppressive forces in this life. People experience oppression when they suffer because they lack the power and the privileges enjoyed by others. Oppression existed at the time of

Jesus just as it does today. The gospels go to great lengths to emphasize Jesus' special concern for those suffering most under the yoke of oppression. If we want to be faithful to Jesus, we must ask ourselves what groups are the most oppressed in our world.

One example of an oppressive situation that can appear to be distant is actually as close as the clothes on our backs. Much of the clothing sold in our shopping malls is produced in what are commonly called "sweatshops." Sweatshops are factories where workers put in long hours in substandard conditions for little pay. Tight regulations make these workers little more than slaves. (Imagine adults living in a guarded compound that is locked at 9:00 PM so that no one can leave or enter.) Ninety percent of sweatshop workers are women. Women work in sweatshops partially because they lack the employment opportunities available to men. Some women, or more accurately young girls, become prostitutes for the same reason. A disproportionate number of women worldwide are numbered among the oppressed.

Jesus himself experienced oppression. As a carpenter in Nazareth, he earned barely enough to stay alive while providing for the needs and desires of the wealthy. Once he publicly proclaimed his message of good news for the poor, he took to the roads, inviting poor and rich, women and men, outcasts and privileged, to live differently. His actions, such as eating with tax collectors and prostitutes, were liberating to those who were oppressed.

Sometimes we can overly spiritualize the message of Jesus, as if our gaze should always be on matters beyond the cares and concerns of this world. Mother Jones, who dedicated her long life to helping workers and forming labor unions, said that we should "pray for the dead and work like hell for the living." A contemporary evangelical Christian reminds us: "No one gets into heaven without a letter of recommendation from the poor."

By speaking out against oppression, Jesus both challenges us and offers us hope. Jesus knew that when some people are oppressed, everyone is oppressed. Women's oppression means men's oppression. Jesus offers us an alternative. Find out where and how people are suffering, and take steps to alleviate their suffering. By working against oppression we stand with Jesus who sets all captives free—including ourselves.

≋ Reflect

- *What feelings did you have when you read about Jesus' stand on oppression? Do you ever pray for the oppressed or for the courage to help them? In what particular ways?*

- *How does Jesus inspire you to get involved with the oppressed? In what concrete ways might you "work like hell for the living"?*

- *What might Jesus be asking you to do or be in your life right now as his follower?*

Your Thoughts

9

Jesus and Women

There were also women looking on from a distance....
These used to follow him and provided for him when he
was in Galilee; and there were many other women
who had come up with him to Jerusalem.
MARK 15:40–41

Fifty years ago, books about Jesus made little mention of women. Today, entire books are written on the subject. Perhaps contemporary writers who explore Jesus' teachings about women are simply trying to be relevant and "politically correct." On the other hand, they may be on to something. Perhaps the question of Jesus and women is not a peripheral one at all but actually goes right to the heart of the Christian message. In his culture, women were among those overlooked and undervalued. Isn't it precisely to those who are overlooked that Jesus preached his message?

In a number of gospel passages, women are mentioned as an afterthought. For instance, at the crucifixion "there were also women" (Mk 15:40). Matthew's gospel says that Jesus fed five thousand people, "besides women and children" (Mt 14:21). Despite being overlooked, women are a surprisingly active presence in Jesus' ministry. They take care of Jesus and are among the faithful disciples who accompany him. In fact, the women have more staying power during Jesus' final days than the male disciples do. Women are specifically mentioned as following so close to Jesus while he carries his cross that he converses with them in their weeping and wailing. Women stay by Jesus during the ordeal of his crucifixion. After he is taken down from the cross, two women friends possess the courage to go see where Jesus is buried. It is the women who first discover the empty tomb on Easter.

Women in the gospels offer us wisdom more through their actions than through their words. One lesson we learn from a woman is that what appears to be little and insignificant is often more important than what seems to be momentous. This lesson is illustrated in the story of Jesus' mother entreating her son to change some containers of water into wine so that a couple's marriage feast is not spoiled. Mary is attentive to the needs of the newlyweds: "They have no wine" (Jn 2:3). She pushes Jesus into an act of compassion; then she instructs the waiters (and us), "Do whatever he tells you" (Jn 2:5).

In another incident, a woman named Mary sits at Jesus' feet while her sister, Martha, cooks a meal. It is an understated story, a simple domestic scene, but it describes two models of Christian discipleship. A striking feature of the story is that women are not confined to the kitchen. In fact, Jesus says that Mary "has chosen the better part" (Lk 10:42). She sits at his feet like a disciple, not a servant. Does Jesus want us to be like Mary instead of Martha? Anyone who has ever come home to a clean house and a home-cooked meal knows that active service is also an expression of holiness. Both Mary and Martha represent models of hospitality and discipleship expressed in Christian homes, homeless shelters, hospitals, and communities. Perhaps Jesus wants all of us to do the work of Martha with the heart of Mary.

Scripture scholars have told us for some time that Jesus treated women with an openness and equality that defied the social conventions of his time. The stories of Jesus and the Samaritan woman, the woman accused of adultery, and the woman who washed his feet with her hair illustrate Jesus' concern for women. As one contemporary writer reminds us, Jesus saw the beauty of God shining as clearly through the face of a prostitute as he did through that of his mother. In his interactions with women, Jesus did not anticipate modern feminist ideology. He simply taught us how to relate to one another.

≋ Reflect

- *How do you feel about the way Jesus related to women in the gospels? In what ways does this help you relate to Jesus in prayer?*

- *Choose a gospel story that includes a woman and read it carefully. Then talk to Jesus in prayer about it. How might this exercise help you "put on the mind of Christ"?*

- *Jesus had qualities of openness and acceptance. How might you imitate these in your daily actions?*

Your Thoughts

10

Stress and Anxiety

*Look at the birds of the air; they neither sow nor reap nor
gather into barns, and yet your heavenly Father feeds them.
Consider the lilies of the field, how they grow; they neither
toil nor spin....Therefore do not worry.*
MATTHEW 6:26, 28, 31

Does your life seem out of control? Do you feel backed into a corner with the walls closing in on you? Are you overwhelmed keeping up with work, social life, family matters, and time for yourself? Is everything okay at home? Are you struggling to balance the responsibilities you have? The many tensions that weigh upon us bring stress. At its worst, stress represents the tip of an iceberg. The real culprit is anxiety's dread that grips when life seems to lack meaning and direction. It is one thing to say, "I can't keep up"; it is another to say, "What's the use?" Stress muddies life. Many Americans are seriously stressed out. Perhaps you are one of them.

By reminding us of carefree birds and peaceful lilies, Jesus wants to relieve our anxiety. Flowers never fret about what to wear to a party Saturday night. No bird says, "I'm anxious about gaining a few pounds. I think I'll skip that worm lunch today." Jesus implies that flowers and birds instinctively realize that the good God, like a loving and all-knowing parent, oversees all. We would do well to come to the same realization. Ultimately, God is in charge, not us.

Jesus does not seem to have been stress-free during his life; he certainly was no poster boy for peace of mind. When he takes time to go into the desert and get away from it all, he ends up wrestling with powerful demons. In fact, right up to his death on the cross Jesus agonized over the problems and the decisions he faced. We call the night before his death "the agony in the garden," and Luke's gospel says that he sweated blood that night. Because he knew the terror of anxiety, Jesus left us two prayers worth repeating during our anxious moments: "My Father, if it is possible, let this cup pass from me; yet not what I want but what you want" (Mt 26:39), and "Father, into your hands I commend my spirit" (Lk 23:46).

What can we do about anxiety and stress? First, we need to recognize when we are under stress. Sometimes stress becomes so commonplace that we fail to realize what it might be like to live without it. Second, we might try some stress management techniques. Jesus reminds us: "Come away to a deserted place all by yourselves and rest a while" (Mk 6:31). Jesus sought moments of prayer, celebration with friends, and quiet time in order to become energized by the Spirit. Finally, we need to recognize the stresses that can be alleviated by decisive action. For instance, if we find that running late for work or school every day brings stress, then we should plan so that we are not late. If certain patterns in our relationships make us anxious, we should take steps to change those patterns.

We can find great relief if we let Jesus in on our anxiety. Jesus was not a holy man sitting above the fray. The dangers that confronted him and the many problems that surrounded him must have caused him anxiety as well.

Despite being under stress himself, however, he had an uncanny ability to be present to the people around him, helping them through their own difficult times. He can be present to us in the same way. After all, he left us these words of comfort: "Come to me, all you that are weary and are carrying heavy burdens, and I will give you rest. For my yoke is easy, and my burden is light" (Mt 11:28, 30). Jesus is yoked with us; he carries our burdens with us. With Jesus beside us, and despite our stresses and the dread we feel, we can be like the birds of the air and the lilies of the field—soaring to new heights and blossoming in beauty.

≋ Reflect

- *What is your stress level right now? What tends to increase stress for you? How does your faith help you deal with this?*

- *When you feel anxious, do you carve out time for quiet prayer and reflection? Do you ever place your worries in the hands of Jesus and talk to him about them? Why or why not?*

- *What words of Jesus do you find worth repeating during times of stress and anxiety?*

Your Thoughts

11

The Gift of Believing

Your faith has made you well; go in peace,
and be healed of your disease.
MARK 5:34

"Do you really believe all this stuff about Jesus?" Sometime we will either say or hear these words. There are actually three parts to this question: 1) believing, 2) all this stuff, and 3) Jesus' connection to this stuff. If we seriously think about it, we will discover that a whole host of very important questions are involved. Do our lives have meaning? Does someone, far beyond our family and friends, and yet never absent from us, love us without question? In the end, will we be sheltered from harm and from annihilation? Does eternal bliss or mere nothingness await us after death? Despite the ever-present realities of evil, suffering, and destruction, are there grounds for hope and for trying to make a difference in the world?

The questions that make up "all this stuff" are pretty important. In fact, they are probably the most important questions we can ask. If we spend our time constantly thinking about them, we might be overcome with anxiety. On the other hand, if we did not ask these important questions, we would not be human. If we have a basis upon which to face these questions, we can go through life with freedom, direction, and purpose.

What does Jesus say about these profound questions that make up our search for meaning? He affirms that the grand picture of a loving, meaning-giving, all-powerful presence holds sway in the workings of the world. Jesus calls the giver of meaning "God"; God's presence he calls "the reign of God." Jesus also lets us in on the mysteries of death and our final end, offering hope and salvation. He does so, not just through his words, but also through his very life. If we ever wonder, "Does anybody really care?" we should find a crucifix and simply gaze upon it for a few moments. The image of Jesus on the cross answers the question with powerful affirmation. Furthermore, when we are in need of hope, we can contemplate the image of Christ who is raised from the dead.

Even if we do accept that Jesus addresses the great questions of life, we still might not believe in him. How can we come to believe in Jesus as Savior of the world when the world seems so unsalvageable? Many people attend religious services exalting Jesus, only to walk out unmoved. The problem is that believing is not something that takes place only in the head; believing is also a matter of the heart. Sometimes words and thinking can be obstacles to a "knowing heart." We often hear faith referred to as a mystery. However, our heart itself—the deep-down core of our being—is mystery as well. Faith means plunging ourselves into the mystery of our very existence and finding that we are not alone there. We need to find our heart and get in touch with where it lies, so we can open it up to Christ.

Questioning represents a holy longing for wholeness. Questioning is not an obstacle to faith when it leads to a realization that life is a profound mystery. Linking together the great puzzling questions of life with Jesus can lead to faith in him, mystery touching mystery. Faith is a transformation of the heart. (So-called "heartless people" are not lacking a heart; rather they encounter obstacles blocking their pathway to the mystery of compassion and peace.)

Blessed with the gift of faith, we will discover that Jesus offers peace and healing, and we will find our broken hearts made whole again.

≋ Reflect

- *Are there "great questions of life" that you find puzzling? How might the gift of faith color your response to these questions?*

- *Have you ever faced a catastrophe that plunged you into the mystery of your existence"? What might this feel like? What insights might you get from prayer?*

- *What is the relationship between doubt and faith for you? Are they contradictory realities? Do you share your doubts with Jesus in prayer?*

Your Thoughts

12

Christmas Spirit

The time came for her to deliver her child.
And she gave birth to her firstborn son and wrapped
him in bands of cloth, and laid him in a manger,
because there was no place for them in the inn.
LUKE 2:6–7

I f we wanted to be Grinches or Scrooges, we could certainly make a case for the dark side of Christmas. It is not surprising that suicides increase during the holidays. In the northern hemisphere, December is a cold and dark time, and daylight is short. (Christmas is celebrated at this time to tap into the natural significance of the winter solstice, when many ancient cultures celebrated the beginning of increased daylight.) Christmas magnifies any emptiness we feel; everything we hear tells us that we are to be upbeat and jolly. We can easily get so caught up in activity—shopping, meal planning, overloading our senses with the artificial sights and sounds of the season—that we miss the simple, pure experience of Christmas. Too often, Christmastime never quite measures up to the hype.

Nonetheless, the birth of Jesus, the "reason for the season," is certainly something to get excited about. Christmas should be a time of sheer joy and not just for children. The gospels of Luke and Matthew contain beautiful stories of Jesus' birth. The evangelists recognize Christ's coming as an event that transformed the world for all eternity. Through touching images, they provide snapshots of what this transformation means.

A bright star announces the coming of the Light of the World that dispels all darkness. Angels cry out, "Peace on earth; good will to all." Lowly shepherds, looked upon as suspect and outcasts, are the first to hear of the Savior's birth. Scholars from the mysterious East, the magi, find their way to Jesus' birthplace, worship him, and give him gifts. These wise ones remind us that people of all nations recognize Jesus as king. Jesus does not arrive in a fiery chariot, like a great king or mighty warrior; he comes into the world just like the rest of us: a helpless baby, needy and vulnerable. Images of sheep and shepherds, stars and heavenly choirs, and a baby fighting off winter's cold tug at our hearts. The Christmas spirit is about following our hearts.

In the classic Christmas movie *It's a Wonderful Life*, the main character is given the opportunity to see what the world would be like if he had not been born. A worthwhile Christmas meditation is to ponder what the world would be like if Jesus had never been born. The only "King of the Jews" at the time would have been Herod, a self-serving and ruthless ruler. Because of the birth of Jesus, we have a very different model of power and leadership.

With the birth of Jesus we encounter a God who is willing to be present in the form of a fragile newborn. We call this Christ-child Emmanuel, meaning "God with us." Without Christmas, God might be viewed as remote and unapproachable, someone to be feared. Instead, we know that the true God emptied himself of all power and majesty for us. The birth of Jesus signals the birth of love beyond human comprehension, a love so complete that God alone can give it.

≋ Reflect

- *What feelings does the experience of Christmas evoke in you? Have you ever thought of it as the feast of "God with us"?*

- *Which images associated with Christmas do you bring to prayer?*

- *What steps might you take to keep a sense of the spirituality of Christmas?*

Your Thoughts

13

The Lord's Prayer

When you pray, say: "Father, hallowed be your name.
Your kingdom come. Give us each day our daily bread.
And forgive us our sins, for we ourselves forgive
everyone indebted to us."
LUKE 11:2–4

D uring the Vietnam War, a Christian American boy fresh out of high school found himself wounded along a riverbank in the jungles of Vietnam. Shrapnel in his legs prevented him from walking. As evening came, he realized that no helicopters would search for him at least until daybreak. Throughout the night he kept repeating the one prayer he remembered, the Lord's Prayer. He was rescued the next day and credits the prayer with saving his life.

Jesus' directions about how to pray are found in the Lord's Prayer, known simply as the Our Father. During the liturgy, we precede its recitation with the words, "We dare to say…." Saying this prayer is taking a great risk; it opens us to some costly ideas. It also spells out God's dream for us.

The prayer begins with an invitation to call God Abba, a more intimate word than "Father." "Daddy" comes closer to its meaning.

Jesus wants us to start our prayer by remembering that God is loving and caring enough to be called "Daddy." The prayer continues by challenging us to conform our world and our will to God's kingdom and God's will.

Next, the prayer gets specific. We ask God to provide daily bread—not extravagance, but the basics to sustain us. Praying this part of the Lord's Prayer expresses our appreciation for God's gifts of food and drink that nourish us. We pray for "our daily bread"—not mine alone but ours. Calling God "our" Father and pleading for "our" daily bread remind us of our relationship both with God and with one another. Finally, we beg for forgiveness. Jesus links God's forgiveness with our attempts at forgiving. Our pleas for release from the burden of our guilt ring hollow unless we can respond with forgiveness to others. To forgive others and ourselves enables us to receive the forgiveness God offers.

If we are like most people, we sleepwalk through the Lord's Prayer. In a sense, inattention does not matter. Prayer is our relationship with God—every aspect of it, not just the words. Prayer means being attentive to God as we go about the daily chores of life. We can pray as we pay the bills, prepare meals, and take out the trash. If we are students, might it make a difference to pray before starting homework?

The Lord's Prayer gives voice to our concerns when we would otherwise find ourselves speechless. If we drive by an accident and notice someone being placed in an ambulance, we have the Lord's Prayer to say. If we visit someone in the hospital who asks for our prayers, we have words to say. Whenever we get stuck about how to make sense of life, we always have the words our Savior gave us. Amen.

≋ Reflect

- *Say the Lord's Prayer slowly and attentively. Imagine that the words are directed to you personally. Explore each phrase of the prayer as if it has something to say to you about God's love.*

- *What kind of prayer is most meaningful for you?*

- *How do you incorporate prayer into your daily routine?*

Your Thoughts

14

The Man Born Blind

As he walked along, he saw a man blind from birth.
He spat on the ground and made mud with the saliva
and spread the mud on the man's eyes….
[The man] washed and came back able to see.
Jesus said, "I came into this world for judgment so that those
who do not see may see, and those who do see may become
blind." Some of the Pharisees near him heard this
and said to him, "Surely we are not blind, are we?"
JOHN 9:1, 6, 7, 39–40

What makes for a good movie? When we walk out of a good movie, we often see things differently from the way we saw things before we went in. The film *Far from Heaven* portrays the subtle racism underlying life in Connecticut in the 1950s. In one scene, black waiters are serving a group of white people at a cocktail party. Those being served barely notice their servers. One white woman sees a black man as an equal, as an intelligent and sensitive man, as a person capable of friendship. All the other whites in the movie are blind to this possibility. They believe that this woman is the one who is blind to the necessity of upholding racial barriers in order to maintain "polite society." The movie forces us to question what it means to be blind and what it means to see.

John's gospel goes to great lengths to describe an incident in which Jesus cured a man blind from birth. Just as in *Far from Heaven*, this story overturns commonly held notions of sight and blindness. By curing a man of his blindness, Jesus ignited a controversy. When some leaders learned of the miraculous cure, they questioned the man's parents, who insisted that their son had been blind from birth. The leaders then questioned the man himself, and he assured them that he was blind before, but now can see. Unable to accept that God is working through Jesus, the leaders were "spiritually blind." They refused to accept that the blind see and the lame walk at Jesus' touch. The formerly blind man was able to see Jesus for who he is —"the Son of Man" (Jn 9:35).

The gospels contain so many accounts of miracles that they are hard to dismiss. Healing is an important dimension of Jesus' ministry and appeal. Jesus cured specific individuals he met who suffered. The miracles also demonstrate a more universal truth: Christ will heal us of our infirmities and relieve our suffering, even if these healings come at death. The greatest cure, now and at the hour of death, is to have our eyes opened to God and God's care for us. Each account of a miraculous cure is the gospel writer saying, "Do you see? Jesus' compassionate healing is a sign of what God wants for each of us."

We all have blind spots. We have times when we realize that we came from God and we are making our way back to God, but often our vision is easily blurred. We may need a jolt to help us see straight.

One way to jolt ourselves is to get involved in some way with people who have obvious needs—not just to be healers but to be healed ourselves by those we serve. The wonder of healing did not end in the first century; we can be instruments of healing today. People who serve others in need often remark that they receive more than they give. To participate in works of healing connects us with Jesus the healer. If you have never been involved with people who are struggling or suffering, try it. You will find it to be an eye-opening experience.

≋ Reflect

- *Have you ever thought of yourself as a healer? Have you ever helped someone who actually helped you more?*

- *What healing do you need from Jesus? How do you express this in your prayer?*

- *How are you an instrument of healing for others?*

✒ Your Thoughts

15

Vocation

Go therefore and make disciples of all nations….
And remember, I am with you always, to the end of the age.
MATTHEW 28:19–20

C hildren frequently are subjected to this question: "What do you want to be when you grow up?" Typically, children answer by naming high-profile professions: professional athletes, musicians, doctors, astronauts. We might feel called to do something with our lives only to hear someone say, "That's not going to make you any money." Jesus pursued a life's work that no mother would choose for her son—to wander about homeless and jobless, responding to the needs of strangers and spending time with unsavory persons.

Christianity has a term for our life's work: vocation. "Vocation" means "calling." Vocation is a deeper, more profound, and inclusive word than "career" or "profession." "Profession" is a neutral term: we are trained to do certain things. ("The drivers in this commercial are trained professionals.") We can look at our livelihoods as either professions or vocations. The distinction makes all the difference in the world.

For example, an athlete who recognizes his or her influence on young people and acts accordingly is a great blessing. Similarly, a teacher who hears from a former student that her teaching left a lasting impression realizes that her work is truly a vocation. Fire fighters and police officers risk their lives, not for their careers, but out of a sense of vocation. Vocation adds a foundation and a purpose to all that we do. Through our actions we have the awesome responsibility of contributing to God's work.

Our vocations manifest themselves throughout our lives and not just in the way we earn our livings. A vocation might simply be a call to be patient and to live a lifetime of searching, or it might be to struggle with overcoming depression or anxiety. There is danger, however, if we do not follow our dreams. Writing of his experiences in the death camps of Nazi Germany, Viktor Frankl observed that the people who struggled most to survive either felt that they had someone waiting for them or that they had a life's work to which they were called. A vocation is always some form of service; it can be a call to be a bartender, a hairdresser, a sales clerk, or a parent. All Christians are called to be ambassadors of Christ, which means "friend makers."

"What would Jesus do?" is sometimes used as the guiding principle for living the Christian life. A more precise question might be "What would Jesus want me to do?" In other words, we each have unique talents and unique vocations. We bring all that we are to all that we do. One of the most important tasks in life is to discover one's vocation, and it is an ongoing discovery. Pursuing a vocation is hard work. The effort we put into schoolwork, housework, paperwork, and simply being a good friend results in a lifelong vocation.

Money is an example of an instrument available to use in the fulfillment of a vocation. Born into a wealthy Philadelphia family, Katharine Drexel found her vocation in part by asking, "What should I do with my money?" We can ask ourselves how we spend our time, our talents, and our treasure. Our vocation is our response to Jesus' call, "Come, follow me."

≋ Reflect

- *What are you being called to do? Have you prayed for guidance to understand this more clearly?*

- *How would people close to you describe your vocation—based on your words and actions?*

- *In what ways do you use your time, talents, and resources for the good of others?*

Your Thoughts

16

Prince of Peace

You have heard that it was said, "An eye for an eye and a tooth for a tooth." But I say to you, do not resist an evildoer. But if anyone strikes you on the right cheek, turn the other also; and if anyone wants to sue you and take your coat, give your cloak as well….
MATTHEW 5:38–40

World War I was the bloodiest war known to history. Often German and English trenches were within shouting distance of each other. Christmas Eve of 1914, the first Christmas of the war, saw an unusual event. First, German soldiers lit candles on Christmas trees, making them possible targets of British bullets. No British soldiers fired their weapons. Next, some men began singing carols, and soldiers from both sides ventured out into the strip of land between their trenches. A Scottish soldier produced a soccer ball, and a game between the two sides ensued. A German barber is reported to have given a British soldier a haircut, and a German juggler performed for the enemy troops. Finally, gifts were exchanged. When generals on both sides heard of this informal Christmas truce, they ordered their soldiers back into their trenches. Steps were taken to prevent such fraternizing by opposing soldiers every Christmas for the remainder of the war.

Jesus knew of war and the causes of war. He lived in a time of intense conflict. The night before his execution Jesus rebuked one of his friends for striking an arresting soldier with a sword. Jesus told his friend point-blank: Put away your sword! On the other hand, Jesus did not avoid conflict. For the three years of his active ministry, he led a very public life. He constantly spoke the truth and accrued powerful enemies in the process. Anyone listening to him may have wondered whether he was pro-Roman or pro-Jewish. Jesus cared both for Jews and non-Jews and even spent time with a Jewish tax collector who worked for the Romans. Jesus focused on the ways people hurt and on what could be done to make their lives better. He did not care about people's nationality; he saw a bigger picture.

The passage from Matthew's gospel about turning the other cheek illustrates how Jesus approached conflict. For many, this statement seems extreme. Nonetheless, there are three implications underlying the words that are worth pondering.

First, the statement is part of a series in which Jesus contrasted the accepted wisdom with his wisdom. In his day, "an eye for an eye" was the accepted position, and it came right from the Bible. By rejecting this principle, Jesus teaches that violence is not sacred. Some people still believe that violence and war are what God wants, and some people hold that, "God is on our side." Jesus did not sanction violence. Do we dare believe that he sanctions violence today?

Second, Jesus urges us to look at the world through the eyes of our enemies. Religious fundamentalists who resort to violence do so because they cannot get into the skin of their enemies. When we experience conflict, we need to search for whatever truth exists in our opponent's perspective. Our tendency in wartime is to demonize our enemies rather than see them as people who care for loved ones and have some moral sense—no matter how distorted.

Third, Jesus urges us to be creative. "An eye for an eye" is not a very creative way to resolve a conflict. It can result in the conflict simmering so that the injured parties on both sides move on to the "tooth for a tooth" phase, and on and on. Rejecting violence means using our imagination and searching for innovative ways to address the conflicts that we face. Violence does not move us toward the world God wants for us; only difficult, painstaking nonviolent strategies do. Is there any question but that the World War I soccer match reflected the spirit of Christ and Christmas more than the generals' call to arms?

≈≈ Reflect

- *Are you experiencing conflict in your life right now? Do you ever discuss conflict with Jesus in prayer? Why or why not?*

- *Have you ever acted as a peacemaker? How did you feel doing this? What was the result?*

- *How are peacemakers looked upon today: as foolish? naive? heroic? signs of hope for a new world?*

Your Thoughts

17

Jesus the Christ

He asked them, "But who do you say that I am?"
Peter answered him, "You are the Messiah."
MARK 8:29

I
n one version of the medieval legend of Sir Launfal, a knight
passes a beggar outside his castle as he sets out in search of the
Holy Grail. Unsuccessful in his quest, he returns battered and
bereft of all his resources only to find the same beggar outside his
walls. When he offers the man his remaining crust of bread, he realizes that the beggar is Christ himself. Christian tradition contains
many such stories reflecting Jesus' message about how he is present
"in the least of these."

Proclaiming Jesus as Christ does not erase his humanity; it ele-
vates our humanity. Ancient formulas of faith say that Christ, one
with the Father, humbled himself in order that we would be exalted.
Sometimes the words "Jesus" and "Christ" are used interchange-
ably, as if they mean the same thing. Jesus' mother Mary (probably
"Miriam" in Hebrew) called her son something like "Yeshua" or
"Joshua." "Jesus" is a Greek version of the Hebrew, and it is the
name by which we know him today. "Christ" is a Greek translation
of Hebrew "Messiah," and means "anointed one."

Ancient rulers were anointed with oil when they took on the role of leading their people. To be anointed was to be chosen, singled out for a special task, marked for life. When Peter declared that Jesus was the Messiah, Peter had in mind the special meaning the title had in Jewish tradition. Jesus was anointed to be Savior of the world. Through the Messiah, the darkness that hung over the world was dispersed.

Invoking the name "Christ" always sends us back to the Jesus we read about in the gospels. This name also invites us to look around and to seek him wherever we are. The glory of Christianity is that Christ overcame the restrictions of time and space; he is both the beginning and the end, not to mention a presence everywhere in between. Paul wrote that distinctions and hostility between Jews and Greeks, slaves and free persons, women and men, should no longer exist. We are all in Christ, and through Christ we have been made one.

Where do we find Christ today? Christian faith tells us that whenever we treat people with gentleness and concern as Jesus did, we are meeting Christ and acting as Christ. Social movements and organizations that work for freedom, equality, and a better life for everybody are an extension of the work of Christ. Christ is present whenever we gather together to pray. When looking at events taking place in our world, friends of Christ always search for him—even when he is hidden from view.

The story of Sir Launfal reminds us not to be surprised if Christ shows up in unlikely places. Paul was not making an observation when he said that in Christ there are no longer slaves and free persons; he was stating an obligation. Christ refers to the person of Jesus in his role as Savior of the world. Paul writes of the Body of Christ, a community of interconnected persons responsible for one another. Because we are connected as members of that body, the way we live our lives reveals our response to Jesus' question, "Who do you say that I am?"

 ## Reflect

- *Where might "searching for Christ in the world today" lead you?*

- *How can you cultivate "Christ-consciousness" in your dealings with others?*

- *If you were asked, "Who is Christ for you?" how would you respond?*

Your Thoughts

18

Children and Play

People were bringing little children to him in order that he might touch them; and the disciples spoke sternly to them. But when Jesus saw this, he was indignant and said to them, "Let the little children come to me; do not stop them; for it is to such as these that the kingdom of God belongs."
MARK 10:13–14

A forecast of snow always sends people scrambling. There is hot chocolate to be bought and boots to be found. One day, a set of parents heard that heavy snowfall was on the way. The father and mother both left work early. On the way home, the mother stopped and bought a snow shovel. The father stopped and bought a sled. This commonplace incident is amusing—except, perhaps, to the mother. The purchase of the sled reflects an important gospel message illustrated in the story of Jesus and the children. For children of all ages, snow means sledding not shoveling. (Perhaps children are on to something about the kingdom of God.)

Unless there is a serious problem, put children in a room and soon they will begin to play—with or without toys. What a great gift it is to play! Playing is a key activity for children. When we play around, we feel childlike once again. Francis of Assisi, viewed by many as the quintessential model of Christ, was known for his playful spirit. According to one story, he often picked up sticks and pretended to be playing the violin while singing songs of joy—in French!

Jesus taught that the kingdom of God belongs to children. Only children and those who can be like them can enter the kingdom Jesus proclaims. In one gospel passage, Jesus welcomes the children, and his disciples are taken aback by his words. In Jesus' day, people debated whether or not children could be counted as persons because children did not work and were not expected to uphold the commandments required for living a good Jewish life.

What makes children so appealing to Jesus? One answer may be that they are particularly vulnerable, and that Jesus' heart always goes out to the defenseless. Another part of the answer may be as simple as: "They play." Often siblings of a child with Down syndrome say that their brother or sister gives them joy. These siblings learn to have fun and to view life with a spirit of playful glee. Those who tried to keep children away from Jesus projected the belief that work decides a person's worth. This attitude made Jesus angry. He knew God's kingdom, and he knew that eternal life with the Father was not measured merely by punching a clock and marking time spent at work. The new life Jesus offers is pure gift, not something earned. If all we do is work, we will feel very uncomfortable in heaven.

What did Jesus have in mind by drawing children to himself and by pointing out how they are models for the rest of us? Unfortunately, many Christians reduce their faith to morality—dos and don'ts (mostly don'ts). They summarize their faith this way: "Being Christian means being good and not doing anything wrong so that we may merit our eternal reward in heaven." Notice the words "doing," "merit," and "reward." The statement links doing (working at something) with reward (payment that is merited through work). By rebuking his disciples for keeping children from him, Jesus affirms not only children, but also child-likeness.

Adults build homes and stately mansions. Children build castles in the sand that wash away with the tide. Both activities are human activities; one is work, the other play. Our inclination is to value work more than play. There is a great lesson to be learned in building sand-castles—and sledding. Take time to play. Reflect on how playfulness, child-likeness, and Jesus' message intertwine. And let it snow.

Reflect

- *Do you feel that you have a childlike heart? In what particular ways do you exhibit this?*

- *Do you approach prayer as play or work? What is your reason?*

- *What aspect of child-likeness would you most want to cultivate in yourself?*

Your Thoughts

19

The Youthful Jesus

Jesus increased in wisdom and in years,
and in divine and human favor.
LUKE 2:52

Alexander the Great became a king at age twenty and began his work of conquering the world and spreading Greek culture. He helped shape the world to this present day. Joan of Arc was a young teen when she put on men's clothes, a suit of armor, and led French troops in battle against the English. Thérèse of Lisieux, known as the Little Flower, was devoted, even as a teenager, to becoming a close friend of Jesus.

Except for one brief incident, we know nothing of the youthful life of Jesus. We can only make suppositions. He was known to be a carpenter, and no doubt worked at carpentry from childhood. Jesus' first turning point, according to the gospels, occurred when he was around thirty. Until then, he lived a humble life and shared time and resources with the 150 or so villagers in tiny, out-of-the-way Nazareth.

At an age when most young people today attend school full-time, Jesus was already working. He probably made tables and wooden utensils and delivered them to the people who ordered them. For us, adolescence is a time to differentiate ourselves from our parents and in the process to discover who we are. Literature about this stage of life makes it sound like we enter adolescence as children and come out the other end as adults. Of course, real life is not that simple.

During his baptism in the Jordan River at the hands of his cousin John, Jesus experienced the presence of the Holy Spirit within him. Jesus gained the wisdom of knowing who he was and the grace of being overwhelmed with God's love. Although the experience certainly signaled a major life change for Jesus, the sensitivity he developed during his teens and twenties prepared him, and he began preaching.

Although we associate adolescence with our teen years, remember two things: we each follow a personal clock, and we never arrive at the end point of our development. Some boys and girls begin dating at age fourteen, others not until much later. One approach is not "more cool" or more adult than the other. Some people stay at one job all of their lives while others constantly try new things. It is worth repeating: each of us operates by a personal clock. What is important is that, whatever our stage of life, we grow in wisdom and grace. Aging comes naturally; wisdom and grace take some effort. It takes wisdom to know who we are. It takes grace to love who we are.

Wherever we are on life's journey, now is the time to look at who we are and where we are going. Now is the time to savor and to be proud. Now is our special time to grow in wisdom and age and grace.

≋ Reflect

- *Picture Jesus as a youth. What do you think he was like? Might you have been friends?*

- *Can you recall any "stepping stone" or "turning point" moments in your life journey so far? What were they and how did they change you?*

- *How would you describe what is distinctive about your ongoing development?*

20

The Power of Speech

Listen to me, all of you, and understand:
there is nothing outside a person that by going in can defile,
but the things that come out are what defile.
MARK 7:14–15

Once a young boy came home from school with a poor report card. His father, drunk at the time, said to his son, "Look at these grades! You're lazy and you're dumb! You'll never amount to anything." As it turns out, the boy worked hard and achieved great success in the academic world. Nonetheless, whenever he failed to achieve at a high level, the boy thought, "My father was right. I am stupid. Now everyone else is finding that out, too."

Words have power. They can build us up or tear us down. Their impact can last a lifetime. Jesus even equates hateful and harmful speech with murder:

"You have heard that it was said to those of ancient times, 'You shall not murder'; and 'whoever murders shall be liable to judgment.' But I say to you that if you are angry with a brother or sister, you will be liable to judgment; and if you insult a brother or sister, you will be liable to the council; and if you say, 'You fool,' you will be liable to the hell of fire." (Mt 5:21–22)

Jesus reminds us that we need to be attentive to the effects of our speech. Our words can be words of comfort, care, and affirmation; our words can also be deadly. Words can defile, making everyone around us feel unclean. Even though cursing is commonplace nowadays, it can still be jarring and demeaning. The words we use in conversation help create an ambiance. What is the ambiance brought about by harsh-sounding language? Striving for loftier speech is a noble endeavor. Words can make us feel attacked and belittled or uplifted. (Never underestimate the power of a genuine compliment, a "Thank you" or "You're welcome.") Words can be an invitation to intimacy or a dagger driving a wedge between people. Words can be authentic or phony, beautiful or crass.

In Mark's gospel, Jesus takes aside a man who can neither hear nor speak. Jesus touches the man's ears and tongue, and they are opened. Imagine being that man—what words would you most want to hear first? What would you want to say the first day that you could speak?

Hearing and speaking are no less precious gifts, even when we possess them all of our lives. John's gospel refers to Jesus as the "word of God." To see and hear Jesus is to see and hear God. Likewise we are Christ's word. The way we use our speech is one indication of how well we are "being" his word. To be Christ's word in the world is quite a responsibility. Jesus alerts us to the power of words. We need to choose them and use them wisely.

≋ Reflect

- *In what ways do you see and hear Jesus in your daily life?*

- *Name a time when you felt the power your words had, either to build up or to tear down. How did you feel? What was the result?*

- *Have you ever felt that you were "being" Christ's word in the world? In what ways?*

21

God of the Poor, God of the Rich

Blessed are you who are poor,
for yours is the kingdom of God.
But woe to you who are rich,
for you have received your consolation.
LUKE 6:20, 24

Walk around the poorest neighborhood you know. Notice the people living there and the condition of the streets and buildings in the area. If there is a church or other place of worship in the neighborhood, stop in or attend services. Next, visit a wealthy area. Take notice of the condition of the streets and buildings. Look for a church or other place of worship to visit.

In most American cities, a stark contrast exists between the poor and wealthy sections of town. Even the prayers of the people in the two sections are probably vastly different. Worshipers in poor churches quite possibly pray that their heat will not be turned off because they were unable to pay their utility bills the past few months. They may pray that their children stay safe, alive, and healthy because their children face constant violence due to the drug trade around them. They may pray that their children stay in school despite the poor condition of the building. Are worshipers in a church in a wealthy area praying about the same things?

Jesus has harsh words for those who are rich. Woe to the rich; blessed are the poor. "It is easier for a camel to go through the eye of a needle than for someone who is rich to enter the kingdom of God" (Mk 10:25). In a story about a great dinner, the rich fail to get it. The rich, the invited guests, do not come to the feast. The rich are involved in their own projects. The feast is then given for "the poor, the crippled, the blind, and the lame" (Lk 14:21). In another parable, Jesus contrasted the fate of a rich man who feasts daily, with that of poor Lazarus, covered with sores, who longs merely for the scraps from the rich man's table. Lazarus dies and is carried by angels to be with Abraham; the rich man goes to Hades where he suffers constant torment. A great chasm separates the rich man's place of torment from the place of comfort enjoyed by Lazarus—a complete turn-around of the chasm that existed between them in life.

In the gospels, the pattern is challenge and censure for the rich and powerful, and comfort and consolation for the poor and powerless. What are we to make of this? One thing we can say is that Jesus cautioned his followers about the temptations that come with being rich. Being rich brings with it the temptation to become isolated from those who are poor and consequently to be insensitive or unresponsive to their plight. One luxury of being rich is separation and distance, living apart from the ragtag and decrepit conditions that the poor face. The Lazarus story certainly warns people who are rich not to view poor people they encounter as annoyances. The story teaches that if the rich fail to help the poor, the rich will not share in the heavenly blessings promised to the poor.

Dividing the world into "us and them" or "haves and have-nots" does not reflect the all-embracing love in the gospels. Jesus wants everyone to delight in all that life has to offer, and he wants those who are poor to share in the world's riches so that they can experience more delight in their lives. Nonetheless it would be untrue to Jesus' message to dismiss his criticisms of the rich and powerful as hyperbole or exaggeration. Riches are abused when they distract those who possess them from active concern for the suffering of others. Both power and wealth can be traps. Jesus offers the rich and the powerful consolation, but also tough love. Jesus offers the poor and the powerless challenge, but also consoling love. Jesus offers everyone the gift of hope.

≋ Reflect

- *In what ways has Jesus offered you hope? How would you describe this gift?*

- *What is your reaction to the story of Lazarus? Do you identify more with Lazarus or with the rich man? Why?*

- *Have you ever experienced personal poverty? When have you witnessed the poverty of others? How did you respond?*

Your Thoughts

22

Christ the King

Pilate…asked him, "Are you the King of the Jews?"
Jesus answered, "My kingdom is not from this world.
If my kingdom were from this world, my followers would
be fighting to keep me from being handed over.
But as it is, my kingdom is not from here."
JOHN 18:33, 36

A story from the Sufi tradition tells of a man who came to a banquet dressed in shabby clothes. He was seated at the bottom end of the table. At one point during the meal, the man left the banquet, returned in royal garb and was seated at the head of the table. The man then took off his clothes and told the host, "Here are my clothes. Obviously it is these that you honor, not me." If a man with tattered clothes, disheveled hair, and unkempt appearance proclaimed that he was a king, we would probably laugh at him. Kings do not look like beggars, and Jesus did not look much like a king.

The beginning of Matthew's gospel mentions that magi search for the newborn King of the Jews, and find a king who was born in a stable instead of in a palace. Jesus is hailed as king in an incident we commemorate on Palm Sunday. The crowd proclaims, "Blessed is the king who comes in the name of the Lord" (Lk 19:38), while Jesus enters Jerusalem on a donkey—not exactly a noble steed for a king. The gospels go to great lengths to distance Jesus from the kings with whom the people are familiar. Nonetheless, Jesus is truly a king, and ironically, Jesus is executed for claiming to be one. The inscription on his cross spells out his alleged crime—claiming to be "King of the Jews" (Lk 23:38).

In the ancient world, kings were viewed as divinely chosen representatives of God. Grand palaces, the trappings of wealth, many horses, and a strong army demonstrated a king's power. Jesus' kingship is not based on signs of power and wealth, but on humility and even on humiliation. Paradoxically, Jesus is a king not by exercising power but by surrendering power. On trial before Pilate, Jesus renounced the weapons of warfare, which he acknowledged were available to him. (In the spirit of Christ, Francis of Assisi forbade his friars the use of horses because he associated them with power, wealth, and the military. The Franciscan missions along California's coast have one day's walking distance between them. The missionaries walked or at most rode donkeys, not horses.)

Jesus proclaimed a model of kingship that flowed from the strength hidden in weakness. Weapons may appear to be an indication of strength. Actually, they frighten and create walls of suspicion between people. The weak possess no obvious weapons and therefore must find other less threatening, more cooperative ways of getting along. The weak are the forgotten ones who do not benefit from the prosperity enjoyed by those close to the centers of power. Jesus offers the weak a new way of life. If the poor are to survive, they must rely on neighborliness and must take care of one another's needs.

Jesus' world-transforming notion of kingship offers us a taste of true royalty. Some of the best teachers struggled in school and thus learned compassion for their struggling students. Members of Alcoholics Anonymous, who have to battle their own weakness, often exhibit great strength in helping others. How can we live out the royal heritage that is Jesus' legacy to us? Our king—riding a donkey, crowned not with precious gems but with thorns—holds the keys to a kingdom more wonderful than any childhood fairy-tale could fancy.

≋ Reflect

- *Do you think of Jesus as a king? Is what ways is he a king for you personally?*
- *What does being part of the reign of God mean to you?*
- *How do you try to live your baptismal call to be a "priest, prophet, and king" in the model of Jesus?*

Your Thoughts

23

The Holy Family

The angel Gabriel was sent by God to a town in Galilee
called Nazareth, to a virgin engaged to a man
whose name was Joseph, of the house of David.
The virgin's name was Mary. And he came to her and said,
"Greetings, favored one! The Lord is with you….
You will conceive in your womb and bear a son,
and you will name him Jesus."
LUKE 1:26–28, 31

We are all in search of family; everyone needs to belong. Sports fans love it when an entire city backs their team. Young people sometimes join gangs to get a sense of family. One gift of the humanity of Jesus is that he, too, has a family. We can learn about Jesus, even from the little information we have about Mary and Joseph found in the gospels. "Like father (and mother), like son" was as true then as it is now.

Joseph placed people's welfare above following the letter of the law. When he discovered that his betrothed, Mary, was pregnant, he did not choose to submit her to the punishment prescribed by law—public stoning. Joseph wanted to quietly divorce her. Only after receiving a divine revelation did he decide to marry her. Joseph followed his dreams and fled to Egypt, thereby saving his infant son from Herod in the process (Mt 2:13–15). Joseph was earthy and commonplace in the best sense of the word. By tradition, he is associated with physical labor and a happy death (presumably he died with Mary and Jesus beside him).

Mary figures more prominently than Joseph in the gospels. She is both humble and strong-willed. Her greatest contribution to Christianity is her gracious acceptance of her role as the mother of our Savior. In so doing, she is recognized as the first disciple. She speaks of her decision to become the Mother of God as bringing down "the powerful from their thrones" and lifting up "the lowly" (Lk 1:52). We may not think of Mary as "political," but the Magnificat (Lk 1:46–55) certainly has political implications. Her "yes" to God is a political act as well as a spiritual one. Mary is often portrayed as taking her dead son's body into her arms and sorrowfully caressing it. She held her son at a time when other family and friends abandoned him, after people mocked him, and the legal system executed him. No wonder that Christians through the ages have looked upon Mary as a warm, caring, and powerful advocate on their behalf.

Like the rest of us, Jesus learned much from his family. His message is not contained in his brief public life. He also speaks to us through the simple domestic life he lived at Nazareth. It is entirely appropriate that the gospels say nothing about his family life, his livelihood, or his friends back home. These aspects of his life are not the stuff of history; the poor are always nameless and overlooked in the history books. However, these hidden aspects of his life are where most of us live our lives.

Day-to-day life with family and friends is holy, despite tensions and struggles. We readily think of churches, convents, and monasteries as holy places. The Holy Family reminds us that sitting around a table talking about the troubles of the day, getting groceries, and helping with homework are holy actions. We can do things to bring out the holiness of family life, such as gathering for a meal and saying grace or offering a nighttime prayer or blessing to close the day. Such little things may seem unimportant, but they are never insignificant. Jesus' family was a holy one. Holiness can be found in our families as well.

≈≈≈ Reflect

- *Have you ever thought of your daily life as holy? Why or why not?*

- *Recall a holy or precious moment with your family or friends— and then say a prayer of thanksgiving for this moment.*

- *What are your dreams for your spiritual growth? What do you hope for in your relationship with Jesus?*

Your Thoughts

24

Foot-Washing

*Jesus got up from the table, took off his outer robe, and tied a
towel around himself. Then he poured water into a basin
and began to wash the disciples' feet and to wipe them
with the towel that was tied around him.*

JOHN 13:4–5

Mother Teresa of Calcutta was universally acclaimed for
her holiness. Her transformation into a world-
renowned figure began when she noticed sick and old
people lying in the gutters of Calcutta awaiting death. She saw
Christ in their faces and wanted, if nothing else, for them to die
knowing someone loved them. She set her sights on quite a task but
did so with such joy that over four thousand women joined her.
Despite the heroic quality of her work, her mission actually represents behavior expected of everyone committed to living the
Christian life. She put into practice one of the identifying character-
istics of Jesus' followers: washing feet.

Most Christians break bread together at least once a week. However,
for Catholics, foot washing happens ritually only once a year, during
Holy Thursday services. Chances are if we asked a group of people
what Christianity stands for, they would not respond, "foot-washing."

The night before his death Jesus explicitly told his followers to perform two duties—break bread and wash feet. To make sure the point was not missed, Jesus himself washed his disciples' feet and instructed them to do likewise. His actions astonished his friends. Jesus, their Lord and Master, bent down before them like a servant, held their feet, poured water over them, and rubbed them clean with a towel. Washing feet was not like washing hands or washing faces. Before shoes and socks, paved roads, "pick up after your dog" ordinances, and indoor plumbing, feet were dirty business. Would even the lowliest slave be required to perform this duty?

Perhaps all the talk of dirty feet makes us squeamish about being friends with Jesus. Dirty feet certainly take the glamour out of discipleship. Imagine what work or school would be like if every morning before the day began everyone took turns washing one another's feet. No doubt everyone would view coworkers and companions differently throughout the day. Of course the very thought is ludicrous and unnecessary, but simply visualizing that scene can help us appreciate the Christian life.

In the physical act of washing feet, we "stand under" others. This Christian practice reminds us that only when we stand under others do we truly "understand" them. Anyone who has ever worked as a waiter, hairdresser, or store clerk knows what it is like to serve another person. By washing the feet of his disciples, Jesus wanted to make sure that we do not make service of others a mere abstraction.

≋ Reflect

- *Imagine that your job is to bathe and care for people in nursing homes incapable of caring for themselves. What would the experience be like for you?*

- *What experiences of serving others have you had? What was it like?*

- *In what practical ways might you serve others in your life as Jesus would serve them?*

25

Jesus and the Eucharist

*While they were eating, he took a loaf of bread, and after
blessing it he broke it, gave it to them, and said,
"Take; this is my body." Then he took a cup, and after giving
thanks he gave it to them, and all of them drank from it.
He said to them, "This is my blood of the covenant,
which is poured out for many."*
MARK 14:22–24

There are some tricks we use when we are trying to sell a house. One trick is to bake bread before potential buyers arrive. The smell of bread baking makes a house feel welcoming and homey. As a Jew, Jesus knew well the smell of fresh-baked bread. Weekly Sabbath meals were not just a way to gain sustenance for the day; they were also religious events. Bread is an important part of the Sabbath meal and an important part of the yearly Passover celebration. It was probably at such a Passover meal that Jesus blessed unleavened bread and wine, gave it to his friends, and charged them to "do this in remembrance of me" (Lk 22:19).

Why did Jesus leave us with bread and wine at a meal as a lasting reminder of him? Wouldn't a special greeting or a secret handshake have done the same? Jesus was not interested in creating new images but in bringing out the full significance of natural, familiar ones. As bread is broken and wine poured out, Jesus told his friends that in the future, a meal in his memory would make his presence real and tangible.

Jesus is the bread of life because he is broken. The bread of the Eucharist cannot be separated from the broken Jesus on the cross. In Catholic churches, eucharistic bread is received with the words, "The Body of Christ. Amen." Receiving the bread is a communion with Christ and with one another. We are Christ's body—no matter how broken we are. Our hunger is never just physical, and we need to be nourished and not "by bread alone" (Mt 4:4). Overeating itself is a symptom that we hunger for something beyond food.

Each of the four gospels includes a story about Jesus feeding a large gathering of people with a few fish and several loaves of bread. The Eucharist is not for us alone. The gifts we receive in the Eucharist are to be shared when we leave church. Pope John Paul II revealed this understanding of Eucharist when he visited Mother Teresa at her home for the dying in Calcutta in 1986. He first accompanied Mother Teresa into the chapel, where they genuflected and prayed before the tabernacle. Then the two of them went into the wards and bent over the men and women suffering and breathing their last breaths. They knew that Christ was present both in the chapel and in their ailing brothers and sisters.

Eucharist means the transformation of bread and wine—and us—into the Body of Christ. The transformation continues when we participate in the eucharistic meal and when we love and serve as Jesus did. Well-nourished by the Eucharist, we go in peace to love and serve the Lord.

≈≈ Reflect

- *When have you felt Christ's presence most strongly? In prayer? In serving others?*

- *Have you ever been conscious of a spiritual hunger within you? What were you hungering for? How did you satisfy this hunger?*

- *What is your attitude toward the Eucharist? Does it nourish you to love and serve others? In what particular ways?*

Your Thoughts

26

The Good Samaritan

*A man was going down from Jerusalem to Jericho, and fell
into the hands of robbers, who stripped him, beat him, and
went away, leaving him half dead. Now by chance a priest
was going down that road; and when he saw him, he passed
by on the other side. So likewise a Levite, when he came to the
place and saw him, passed by on the other side. But a
Samaritan while traveling came near him; and when he saw
him, he was moved with pity. He went to him and bandaged
his wounds, having poured oil and wine on them.*
LUKE 10:30–34

I n a cartoon, a child holding crayons and a coloring book looks
up at the sky through a string of electric wires. The caption reads,
"See. God doesn't stay inside the lines either." Perhaps the child
in the cartoon is thinking about Jesus' story of the Good Samaritan.

In the first century, Samaritans were not part of Jewish society.
The ancestors of Samaritans were Jews who intermarried with non-
Jewish neighbors and accepted some of their "pagan" ways. To
those Jews who wanted purity at all cost, Samaritans were tainted.
Samaritans were not within the boundaries of what was acceptable
and respectable.

One of Jesus' stories features a Jew and a Samaritan—an odd couple if ever there was one. The Jewish man heads out from Jerusalem. While on the road he is attacked by thieves and left to die. Two pillars of Jewish society pass by but leave the man unattended. Then a Samaritan comes upon the dying man. In the Jewish man's mind, this could only spell trouble. Jews didn't like Samaritans, and vice versa. Jews typically called Samaritans "dogs." In the story, the Samaritan helps the man by taking him to an inn to recover. The Samaritan asks the innkeeper to take care of the man, and promises that on his return trip he would reimburse the innkeeper for his troubles. The commonly accepted interpretation of this parable is that people should be neighborly—"Good Samaritans." Some hospitals bear the name. There are even "Good Samaritan laws" stating that not helping someone in obvious need may result in legal penalties.

There is another meaning in the story when it is stripped of its moral commentary. Jesus is saying, "don't stay within the lines." Jesus looks behind images and impressions. A person's goodness is not determined by perception; goodness is God-given and then shaped and formed by actions. Some Jews labeled all Samaritans evil, misguided, and unclean, and therefore to be avoided at all cost.

Jesus' story nudged his listeners and us to look outside the lines when encountering others. Unfortunately, there are too many incidents in which narrow-mindedness leads to tragedy. For instance, the film *Hotel Rwanda* tells the tragic story of the massacre of 800,000 people in the mid-1990s, a situation that came about because some Rwandans viewed other members of their society as "cockroaches" and expendable.

Who are the Samaritans in our lives? Are there individuals or groups we label in a negative way and thereby close the door to the grace and richness that surely is in them? Do we tend to confine reality within the lines of our limited view?

Education is one way to help expand our vision. True learning always brings disruption to our perspective. One goal of education is moving us along from point A (our previous perception) to point

B (new insights into reality). Do we try to expand our horizons? Jesus' Good Samaritan story asks more of us than simply to be good neighbors. Jesus wants us to enter the world of losers, outcasts, and strangers, and to be open to surprise. The next time we find ourselves about to shut down on someone we find irritating, we might consider thinking "outside the lines."

≈≈≈ Reflect

- Can you think of ways that Jesus acted "outside the lines"?

- What are some ways that you might think or act outside the lines?

- Describe a time when you were delightfully surprised by a spiritual experience. How did this affect you? Did it help you to think about and see others through Jesus' eyes?

Your Thoughts

27

A Double-Edged Sword

Do you think that I have come to bring peace to the earth?
No, I tell you, but rather division!
LUKE 12:51

E xperts on group interaction report that people's faults are frequently also their greatest strengths. For instance, someone
in a group might say about one of the members, "He seldom
speaks up and contributes little to the group" (negative). Someone
else might say of the same person, "He listens quietly and allows
others more time to talk about themselves" (positive). The same
behavior is described first negatively and then positively. There is a
dual nature to our character traits. They are double-edged—negative and positive. Life tends to be that way.

The portrait of Jesus that emerges from the gospels is double-
edged. We read along and conclude that Jesus advocates peace. Then
we discover a passage in which Jesus says that he brings division, not
peace. We read many passages about love but on occasion find harsh
words from Jesus as well. We might like Jesus to be more consistent
and less confusing. When he says that salt that has lost its flavor

should be thrown out, does he mean us? Since he talks so much about God's abiding love, his warnings feel all the more jarring.

To understand this two-sided dimension of Jesus we might step away from him and think about our times and about the people in our lives. Do we know anyone who is all sweetness and light, who would never criticize or question or raise her voice in protest? During a crisis a more forceful approach is called for than sweetness. Tough times call for tough responses. Jesus lived in a time of crisis. He knew firsthand how desperate people were for signs of hope. He saw the suffering around him and was deeply disturbed by it. So many people in power were caught up in minor concerns and ignored or added to the suffering of others. They were, at best, salt without flavor, lamps hidden under baskets. To Jesus, they needed a jolt, something to open their eyes to the dead-end policies they were advocating. Jesus' message is often difficult because he comforted the afflicted while afflicting the comfortable.

The gospels contain great words of comfort. Read the second half of John's gospel if you need reassurance that God loves us entirely. However, the gospels are also laced with words of challenge and confrontation. They are not directed at the "others"—the bad guys—they are directed at us. Our task is to identify the great challenges that face us. In the face of these challenges, what disturbing words does Jesus have for us? What is the "Jesus challenge" we face? What problems in our world would Jesus be speaking about to us? Where would traveling with Jesus lead us?

≈≈≈ Reflect

- *How do you incorporate both the comfort and the challenge of Jesus?*

- *What is the greatest "Jesus challenge" you face?*

- *What are some personal qualities you possess that have both positive and negative dimensions to them? Do you bring these qualities to your prayer?*

28

The Forgiving Jesus

*Now all the tax collectors and sinners were coming near
to listen to him. And the Pharisees and the scribes were
grumbling and saying, "This fellow welcomes sinners
and eats with them."*
LUKE 15:1–2

A successful, well-liked high school girl met with her counselor and told her, "If people really knew me, they wouldn't like me." As the girl revealed her deep, dark secrets, it became clear to the counselor that her guilt and shame did not derive from decisions she had freely and consciously made. Instead, this girl carried within her a host of experiences that she kept hidden that constantly burdened her and left her with a lingering feeling of unworthiness. If this innocent young woman needed consolation, how much more do the rest of us need to hear, "Your sins are forgiven"?

Christian tradition gives a prominent role to the concept of sin. Christianity warns of its glamour and allure. We may have the sense that sin is natural and that it takes supernatural effort to resist it. Or we may think that if we were not restricted by Christianity and conscience, we would have a lot of fun sinning. When Jesus spoke of sin, he almost always referred to it in terms of forgiveness. He did not emphasize punishment, although he made dire predictions about those who stubbornly continued sinning. He viewed sin, not as freedom, but as a crippling constraint.

Neither Judaism nor Jesus nor Christianity invented sin. Jesus acknowledged its existence and the devastating effects it has both on the sinner and on the "sinned against." Jesus wants us to know both that our sins are forgiven and that we are to sin no more. Jesus offers forgiveness "seventy times seven times" and expects us to offer the same—even when it involves forgiving ourselves. Seventy times seven means endless forgiveness. His words on sin are reassuring words, consoling words, freeing words.

The people Jesus is most frustrated with are those who refuse to recognize their sinful ways and see themselves as above the rest of struggling humanity. In one gospel story, Jesus contrasted a Pharisee and a tax collector. The Pharisee reminded God about all the wonderful deeds he had done. The tax collector simply said, "God, be merciful to me, a sinner" (Lk 18:13). The tax collector sinned and acknowledged it. The Pharisee appeared sinless—he did all the right things—but his attitude was sinful. Instead of connecting with others, he set himself above them. Jesus wanted the Pharisee to turn around and hold hands with the tax collector so that they could bolster each other's resolve and overcome their shortcomings together.

The overriding message of the gospels is love, not condemnation. A story about the seventeenth-century saint, Margaret Mary Alacoque, reinforces this message. (She was instrumental in promulgating the popular Catholic devotion to the Sacred Heart of Jesus.) Margaret Mary was a nun who claimed to have visions of Christ. Local church leaders did what they could to convince her that she was suffering from delusions. To test the validity of her visions, a local priest told Margaret Mary to ask Christ to name his (the priest's) sins. She reported that during his next appearance Christ simply answered, "I don't remember any of his sins."

These words from the compassionate heart of Christ, who looks beyond our sinfulness, are meant for us as well. Our sinfulness enhances rather than diminishes the message of God's love. The guilt and shame we carry within us make us fit receptacles for God's love. Ask God for forgiveness and freedom and the strength to change. God has already granted this request.

≋ Reflect

- *Have you ever felt, "If people really knew me, they wouldn't like me"?*

- *Do you believe that Christ loves and forgives you? What does it feel like to be forgiven?*

- *How does it make you feel to know that Jesus doesn't remember any of your sins?*

🖋 Your Thoughts

29

The Giver of Life

I came that they may have life, and have it abundantly.
JOHN 10:10

A great fear for many people, especially the young, is boredom. Heaven forbid that life becomes dull! Despite being surrounded by endless gadgets designed for our entertainment, we often do find life boring. The music we listen to sounds the same after a while. Movies and television shows seem stuck on four or five plot themes and rarely venture off the beaten path—unless it is crass or absurd. If we do not pay attention, our lives can blend into a bland sameness. Parties lack the luster they had when we were young. Even the Internet, which offers endless venues for new information and contact with others, can leave us wanting more from life.

Part of the problem lies in how we spend our time. We may rely on entertainment to overcome boredom. Henri Nouwen points out that the root of the word means something like "what we do in between the time we engage in living." Entertainment means taking a break from life, not entering into life deeply and passionately. Entertainment is for spectators, not participants. Entertainment is not meant to substitute for living any more than watching a weather forecast on television matches the thrill of being out in an invigorating snowstorm.

Is there an anti-boredom message in Jesus' teachings? He tells us that he wants life for us—life in abundance. How might we move in the direction of full lives? We find hints about what Jesus means by "fullness of life" in his own life. Jesus was extremely attentive to the people around him. He faced plenty of distractions, crowds of people seeking to be healed and people determined to trip him up if he made what they considered to be a false step. Despite the distractions, he saw beauty that others overlooked: in foreigners and children, in tax collectors and penniless widows. He also felt people's pain. Perhaps his ability to enter the lives of others as if their lives were his own provides a key into the fullness of life he offers.

The Trinitarian nun, Sister Peter Claver Fahy, lived this message. She died in 2004 at the age of 105. Into her late nineties she regularly visited people in prisons, taught them to read, and assisted them in their spiritual needs. She always left her friends in prison with the words, "I will carry you in my heart." Spending herself for others kept recharging her enthusiasm for life and sustained her for over a century.

Boredom and depression are powerful psychological forces. Some of us battle these forces more than others. While boredom dulls the pain that comes with life, it also deadens the excitement that entering into life can bring. Boredom's mantra is "There's nothing to do." Life in the Spirit rejoices in all there is to do, leaving in God's hands all that we must leave undone. We view life as boring when we are spectators rather than participants. At death's door we can either say, "I stayed on the sidelines," or "I gave myself to life with Jesus." Jesus urges us to get in the game. We will find him there, offering us life in abundance.

 ## Reflect

- *Do you ever experience boredom? What is it like? What do you tend to do about it?*

- *Have you ever experienced "life in the Spirit"? If not, what might you do to experience this?*

- *How much of a struggle is it for you to be a participant rather than a bystander? What obstacles do you face?*

Your Thoughts

30

Why Does God Allow Suffering?

Righteous Father, the world does not know you,
but I know you; and these know that you have sent me.
I made your name known to them, and I will make it known,
so that the love with which you have loved me
may be in them....
JOHN 17:25–26

There is a play about a group of rabbis confined in a Nazi concentration camp during World War II. The rabbis decide to put God on trial. They submit the evidence against God: God allows babies and children to die. Good people suffer at least as much as bad people do. God does not intervene to protect persecuted people, like themselves—Jews in the genocidal program of the Nazis. Why does God allow people whose entire lives are pain-filled to exist in the first place? After hearing the case against God, the rabbis declare God guilty of cruel and inhuman behavior.

When people of faith lose someone close to them, typically they react in one of two way: some people have their faith shaken; others find their faith is deepened. Look at the world from the perspective of the first group: we pray to God and expect results. We believe that Jesus cares and wonder why he does not show it. If bad people suffer, that is one thing; good people deserve good things to happen to them. Kindly grandfathers should not die lingering deaths. A classmate should not contract a terminal illness or die in a car crash. People should not perish in terrorist attacks because they go to work on a particular day.

Searching the gospels for answers to these questions, we find that Jesus does not provide any. Although he and the Father are one, and despite the great compassion he showers on the sick and the dying, Jesus does not explain suffering. He accepts it as a part of the human condition. Suffering and death remain a mystery. The point of the gospels is that Jesus himself takes on these mysteries, endures them, and in the end, rises triumphantly over them. Faith in the risen Christ does not alleviate suffering and death or uncover their mysteries. Faith in the resurrection gives us hope that life extends beyond death for those we love.

Faith in Christ Jesus does not mean passive acceptance of suffering either. We have our part to play. In the movie *Oh, God*, God is portrayed as an old man who reveals who he is to a grocery store clerk. God asks the clerk if he has any questions for him. The clerk replies, "Why don't you do something about hunger and poverty and the other evils that humans face?" God answers, "I did do something. I made you." This exchange speaks to Christian faith and the mystery of suffering and death. Jesus wants people to be awash in his Father's love for them. He also prays that the Father's love will be present in and through them. Jesus says that this is why he was sent. God does not abandon the sorrowing; sometimes we must look deep to see God's love at work. God is present to the grieving, and sometimes we are the ones chosen to convey the message.

 **Reflect**

- *How does the reality of suffering—a young person's death, terrorist attacks, natural disasters—influence your understanding of God?*

- *What do you think Jesus' message says about suffering and pain?*

- *What is a good prayer to say during a time of physical and emotional suffering?*

Your Thoughts

31

Jesus and Anger

*In the temple he found people selling cattle, sheep, and doves,
and the money changers seated at their tables. Making a whip
of cords, he drove all of them out of the temple, both the sheep
and the cattle. He also poured out the coins of the money
changers and overturned their tables.*
JOHN 2:14–15

H ave you ever been so angry that you said things you later
regretted? Have you ever smashed things or harmed yourself or others out of rage? Have you been known to flip
out when things fail to go your way, when children, parents, or
your spouse does not do your bidding? Anger is a strong emotion,
and it seems to have destruction built into it. If we opened the
gospels for the first time, we might be shocked to read that Jesus
himself displays anger. Although he drew people to himself, he
also angered people, and on occasion expressed anger. Christian
tradition lists anger among the deadly sins. Modern psychology
clarifies how anger is destructive. Anger itself is not sinful. Anger is
sinful only when we express it in unhealthy or harmful ways. In
other words, anger is not good or bad; what we do with our anger
makes the difference.

Jesus expressed anger when he encountered people buying and selling things in the temple. We can imagine the scene. A spiritual aura should prevail in a house of God. Instead, the sound of merchants hawking their goods drowned out the temple quiet. Jesus overturned the tables of the money changers, sending coins flying. He fashioned a whip out of rope and frightened off the merchants and their cattle and sheep. The gospel writer then says that Jesus did these things because of his zeal for his Father's house. "Zeal" means determination, fervor, and passion. It is something quite different from putting a fist through a wall. Being zealous means caring so strongly that we put ourselves on the line, to the point of expressing frustration in forceful ways.

An important question about this incident is: Were Jesus' actions destructive? Was he violent? The story intends to show Jesus' determination in carrying out his Father's work. Jesus decried the lack of holiness in the sacred place. Merchants viewed the temple as a place to do business rather than as God's house. Buyers and sellers were intent on getting what they could from each other. No doubt overturning tables and driving out the animals would have caused quite a stir but little actual damage. By expressing his righteous anger, Jesus called for the restoration of temple holiness and reverence for God and all things sacred.

Denying anger or repressing it does not work. Controlling anger is necessary. It is even possible to befriend anger, making it an ally by channeling its energy. Exploring what is behind anger is also beneficial. If we are regularly angry with a parent or a spouse, perhaps our anger reveals our own frustration level rather than the tendency of parents and spouse to be frustrating. On the other hand, we should be angry that some children today are forced to be soldiers or are sold into slavery. It is important to get angry at hunger and injustice. Anger can lead to destructive and hurtful actions or it can help us cultivate zeal. Choose zeal.

 **Reflect**

- *What do you do with your anger? Have you ever actually befriended it? What was the result?*

- *Imagine the scene in the temple. As a friend of Jesus, how do you feel about his anger?*

- *Have you ever felt righteous anger? How did you display it? What was the result?*

Your Thoughts

32

The Beatitudes

Blessed are you who are poor, for yours is the kingdom of God. Blessed are you who are hungry now, for you will be filled. Blessed are you who weep now, for you will laugh. Blessed are you when people hate you, and when they exclude you, revile you, and defame you on account of the Son of Man. Rejoice on that day and leap for joy.

LUKE 6:20–23

I f you have a chance, read about Pier Georgio Frassati and Jean Donovan. Actually, you may already know people like them— young persons filled with exuberance who spread happiness wherever they go. Both of these saintly people died young, and yet they lived life with a contagious cheerfulness and joy. Both Pier and Jean came from relatively well-off families but distinguished themselves by living with and for people who were poor. Pier Georgio, an Italian who died of polio at age twenty-five in 1925, was an avid mountain climber and skier. The American Jean Donovan drove a motorcycle to work. She later went to El Salvador as a missionary and was murdered for her work there. From his deathbed, Pier Giorgio signed an insurance policy for a poor family and sent a box of medicines to another family in need. Jean went to El Salvador to help poor children and their families and could not bring herself to leave them, even though she knew her life was in danger.

Two gospels contain lists that turn what we normally think of as happiness upside down. The Beatitudes, a longer version in Matthew (5:1–12) and a shorter one in Luke (6:20–23), illustrate the baffling nature of Jesus' teachings. Most people do not view being poor, hungry, or under verbal attack as blessings, yet that is the message of the Beatitudes. The case can be made that Beatitudes get to the heart of the entire Christian message.

How can poverty, hunger, weeping, and persecution be blessings? Put another way, what are we missing if we fail to experience these things? If we are not poor to some degree or in some fashion, then we have no need for anything or anyone. Only those in touch with something lacking can be open to the "holy longing" for God. Poor to the extreme, hungry people constantly hope for more and better things to come. Only those who weep know the pain and suffering that cry out for healing for themselves and others. Those who are reviled and defamed experience the isolation that brings with it a longing for a caring community. In other words, the Beatitudes of Jesus describe people who experience the human condition whole-heartedly with both its lacks and its longings.

The Beatitudes are Jesus' promises to us. Weep now, later we will laugh. Empty now, later we will be filled. Put down now, later we will be raised up. If we are blessed enough to know Jesus—what he has done, what he stands for, what he promises—we will leap for joy. The hardships we face are passing. The Son of Man has entered into them with us and has conquered them. Both Pier Georgio Frassati and Jean Donovan found their joy deepened rather than dampened by sharing their lives with other "people of the Beatitudes."

The Beatitudes are often presented as an agenda for action—almost as if they update the Ten Commandments. The Beatitudes say more about who we are than about what we should do; they describe attitudes for Christian living. As with everything in the

Christian life, the Beatitudes are meant to be shared experiences. Christ does not bring comfort and healing in isolation. Christ operates in us and through us. Despite our own inadequacy and fear of embarrassment, the Beatitudes call us to feed the hungry, bring laughter to the sad, and include the excluded. The Beatitudes are Jesus' affirmation that none of our efforts are in vain. The kingdom of God, promised to the poor, awaits us.

≋ Reflect

- *What do the Beatitudes mean to you?*
- *Which Beatitude speaks most strongly to you? Which Beatitude seems the most difficult for you?*
- *Which blessing from Jesus would you most ask for in prayer? Why is it important to you?*

✐ Your Thoughts

33

Jesus and the Earth

And he said to them, "Go into all the world and
proclaim the good news to the whole creation."
MARK 16:15

Something truly wonderful would be missing from the gospels without references to plants, animals, and the earth itself. Where would we be today if not for the animals that kept Jesus warm in the stable at his birth? Could we appreciate the importance of Jesus' death and resurrection without the images of "a lamb led to slaughter" and a grain of wheat that dies and is buried in the earth so that it can bear much fruit?

We may not immediately link Christianity with environmental concerns. However, Francis of Assisi, recognized as the person who most strongly reflects the image of Jesus, is the patron saint of the environment. Jesus was certainly attentive to the things of the earth. He pointed out that we have much to learn from our non-human sisters and brothers. The gospels do not mention if Jesus had a pet while growing up, but certainly both domestic and wild animals were a constant presence. The earth's gifts of food and drink were also companions during his journey. Grain and fruits were cultivated near the village where Jesus lived.

When we think about the earth today, the first thing we may think of is the environmental crisis. Given the state of the planet, perhaps it should be the first thing that comes to mind. There was something of an environmental crisis in Jesus' day as well. This crisis was not centered on our current concerns, that is, the effects of our misuse and overuse of the earth's limited and fragile resources. Jesus was concerned instead about why so many people lacked the basic necessities and why the goods of the earth were so unfairly distributed. He was concerned about how the have-nots could pool their limited resources and organize themselves to stay alive. These concerns reveal quite an environmental crisis!

The gospels hint that care for the earth and its creatures is part of Jesus' vision of things. Jesus instructs his disciples to "proclaim the good news to the whole creation" (Mk 16:15). In other words, Jesus intends his message for everyone and everything—all creation. He calls upon the strong and the powerful to serve and protect the weak. Animals and plants, like human beings, have inherent value separate from the profit they bring. Perhaps when Jesus overturned the tables of merchants selling doves for sacrifice in the temple, he was, in part, honoring the inherent value of the doves.

Jesus' compassion spreads far and wide, excluding nothing. God is revealed in and through the stuff of the earth. In this twenty-first century, we need to discover anew how to be compassionate, or at least neighborly, to all other manifestations of God's creation.

≋ Reflect

- *Have you ever thought of Jesus as caring about the natural world? Why or what not?*

- *What are some changes you might make so that your lifestyle more closely reflects Jesus' compassionate concern for nature?*

- *When and how do you spend time with nature? Do you ever bring nature into your prayer?*

34

Mother Jesus

"How often have I desired to gather your children together
as a hen gathers her brood under her wings…."
MATTHEW 23:37

The medieval English mystic Julian of Norwich used an intriguing image for Jesus. She called him "Mother Jesus." In so doing, she associated Jesus with the traditional qualities of a mother. The good mother brings us to life and nurtures us. Like Jesus' mother, she remains steadfast in her love through good times and bad. She is sweetness and tenderness. Her concern is for her children, not for herself. Rather than being overbearing and demanding, she is a constant, caring, affirming presence. These qualities sound like ones we associate with Jesus.

In recent times there has been a debate about whether or not to use female images when referring to God. Jesus calls God "our Father," not "our Mother." Wouldn't we diminish the power of that title if we began the Lord's Prayer with "Our Mother," or worse yet, "Our Parent"? The overriding image of God in Scripture is male— Father and (male) Creator. Who are we to dismiss this tradition? God the Father is essential to Christian teaching about the Holy Trinity. We are baptized and bless ourselves in the name of the Father, the Son, and the Holy Spirit.

But wait, others say. No image of God fully captures God's mystery. To reduce God to one image is to engage in idolatry—a violation of the commandments if ever there was one. We should not allow the limitations of our language to limit our conception of God; God is "the name beyond all names," as Muslims say. Though our minds can only think in terms of he, she, or it, God is beyond such limiting categories. The Bible specifies that both women and men are created in God's image. In fact, Jesus uses a feminine image to refer to himself, saying that he is a mother hen who gathers her children under her wings to shelter them from danger.

Tapping into the array of images surrounding him, Jesus displays a colorful and open-minded imagination. He proclaims himself to be the true vine, life-giving water, and a mother hen. Meditating on these and other images for Jesus can help us appreciate his teaching.

These images also remind us to apply the same lively, non-prejudicial imagination to ourselves and to others. If we limit others to stereotypes about what it means to be men or women, we diminish the fullness of their humanity. Sexual stereotypes are even more damaging when we try to fit ourselves into them. There is, however, constant pressure to conform to stereotypes and to view the world in terms of them. ("Real men…[fill in the blanks]." "Girls and women should…[fill in the blanks].")

By referring to himself with images that are female and male, human and non-human, Jesus moves us beyond narrow, limiting notions of God. Jesus is more than any single image can describe; a world of images is available to help us understand him. No description or characterization explains us adequately either. Each of us reflects the unfathomable image of Jesus Christ, who himself is one with the mystery beyond imagining—God.

 **Reflect**

- *What are some images that speak to you of God?*
- *How does the name "Mother Jesus" strike you? What does it suggest about Jesus as a person?*
- *What is your own image of Jesus? What name for him best describes how you feel about him?*

Your Thoughts

35

The Passion of Christ

This is my blood of the covenant,
which is poured out for many.
MARK 14:24

On February 12, 2005, a seventy-three-year-old nun from Dayton, Ohio, named Dorothy Stang was shot at point-blank range in the rainforests of Brazil. She had lived there for twenty-two years. She helped landless farmers and tried to preserve the forests from being destroyed by large ranchers and loggers. She knew of the death threats against her; she had recently reported them to the authorities. She was more concerned about the threat to life experienced by local peasants who were trying to make a modest living through sustainable farming methods. What was a nun from Ohio doing in such a place? Why would she risk her life? One answer she might give is, "I'm helping my sisters and brothers in need." Another answer that would be equally true is, "I'm following in the footsteps of my Lord and Savior, who also gave his life blood for such as these."

Jesus on the cross is a central Christian image rich in symbolic power. The passion accounts of his death and the events preceding it were the first part of the gospel to be written. One early Christian writer refers to the cross as the center of the universe. From the cross the arms of Jesus stretch out to embrace the entire world. His suffering and death are his sacrifice whereby he welcomes all people into his kingdom, a kingdom greater than death.

We do injustice to the cross if we dismiss the excruciating pain and suffering Jesus went through during the ordeal of his crucifixion. (The word "excruciating" comes from the Latin for "cross.") His torment was even deeper than his physical pain. In Mark's gospel, Jesus appears to have fallen into the depths of despair, crying out just before his last breath, "My God, my God, why have you forsaken me?" (15:34). The sacrifice that Jesus made on the cross was complete; he emptied himself in every sense of the word. Despite the controversies surrounding the film, Mel Gibson's *The Passion of the Christ* certainly succeeds in reminding us that the torture Jesus endured was gruesome. (The film does lack any suggestion about how to walk in Jesus' footsteps.) The utter finality of the cross makes the Resurrection all the more remarkable.

Unfortunately, many people are still subject to horrible acts of cruelty today. Sister Dorothy is not the only person killed for trying to make a difference. Eyewitnesses to the murder of Sister Dorothy report that when she was confronted by the *pistoleiros* bent on taking her life, she immediately reached into her bag and pulled out her Bible and began reading to them. What might she have chosen to read, standing before gunmen about to take her life? If her life's work is any indication, she probably tried to remind the men that God stands with the poor and that they should renounce violence against them. If, however, she found her way to the account of that most human experience of Jesus, the giving up his life on the cross, hopefully it gave her courage and comfort before she died.

As we sacrifice to live the Christian life, it is a great blessing to know that our Lord and Savior shares in our suffering and our bouts of despair. Even when death overtakes us, we can say with Jesus, "Father, into your hands I commend my spirit."

 ## Reflect

- *What emotions are stirred in you as you listen to the story of Jesus' passion and death?*

- *What meaning does Christ's suffering and death have for you personally?*

- *Do you believe that Jesus shares your suffering? Are you able to pray with him: "Father, into your hands I commend my spirit"? Why or why not?*

Your Thoughts

36

Christ Is Risen!

Mary Magdalene and the other Mary went to see the tomb.
And suddenly there was a great earthquake; for an angel of
the Lord, descending from heaven, came and rolled back the
stone and sat on it. But the angel said to the women,
"Do not be afraid; I know that you are looking for
Jesus who was crucified. He is not here;
for he has been raised, as he said."
MATTHEW 28:1–2, 5–6

A painting by Eugène Burnand portrays two men with windswept hair hastening toward an important destination. Their look is one of excitement, anticipation, hope-beyond-hope. It is Easter Sunday. The two men are the apostles Peter and John racing to the tomb of Jesus. They placed all their trust in Jesus, but he had been brutally executed just days before. Some women friends astounded the men with the news that the tomb was empty. Could this possibly be true? The younger man, John, clutches his hands. The older man is wide-eyed and on the verge of tears. Peter marvels that Jesus, who had assured his friends that he would rise from the dead, might actually fulfill his promise. At his death Peter had abandoned Jesus; now he hoped that Jesus even in death had not abandoned him. Before Jesus' death, Peter said to him, "You have the words of eternal life" (Jn 6:68). Could the new life they had tasted during their time with Jesus be greater than death itself?

The world is filled with wonderful stories. Is any more wonderful than the story of Jesus raised from the dead? We want our movies to have happy endings—the earth saved from alien invaders, two people finding each other and living happily ever after. We want our lives to have happy endings as well. The story of the Resurrection is one of fulfillment, darkness turned to light, and of everlasting bliss. This story goes beyond all happy endings. No wonder Paul calls the Resurrection the lynchpin holding Christianity together. Without the Resurrection, the Christian story falls apart.

The meaning of the Resurrection is not easily understood—especially confined as we are to limited human language and thought. Resurrection does not mean that Jesus' body was restored to the way it was before he died, as if he had what we might call a "near-death experience." Jesus truly experienced death, as each of us will. On the other hand, Jesus is not a ghost. The Christian creed declares that Jesus rose from the dead, body and soul. After the Resurrection, Jesus is different but not distinct from who he was prior to his death. Post-Easter accounts of Jesus describe a different kind of bodily presence. He spent time with his friends for brief periods, bodily present to them. Then, according to Luke's gospel, he withdrew from them and ascended into heaven, body and soul.

What message does the Resurrection hold for us? The story of Jesus is our story. Jesus did not rise from the dead for himself but for all humanity. The fabric of our being, woven over a lifetime, does not unravel with death. New life awaits us. Because Jesus rose from the dead, the stories of our lives and the lives of our loved ones have happy endings. Life with Christ is available to us now. Thanks to the Resurrection, life with Christ does not end with death. Life is changed, not ended. Alleluia!

 Reflect

- *What Easter images (i.e., crocuses pushing up through the snow, the rising sun) speak most strongly to you?*

- *In what ways does the Christian story of new life following death hold special meaning for you?*

- *The resurrected Christ calls you "friend." How do you feel about this? How might you deepen your faith in his friendship?*

Your Thoughts

Epilogue

Who will separate us from the love of Christ?
Will hardship, or distress, or persecution, or famine,
or nakedness, or peril, or sword?
I am convinced that neither death, nor life,
nor angels, nor rulers, nor things present,
nor things to come, nor powers, nor height, nor depth,
nor anything else in all creation,
will be able to separate us from the love of God
in Christ Jesus our Lord.

ROMANS 8:35, 38–39